CARLA'S
NORDBY

LETTING
~ GO ~

Other Scholastic titles you may enjoy:

LETTING ~GO~

Mary Woodbury

Cover by
Gordon Weber

Scholastic Canada Ltd.

Scholastic Canada Ltd.
123 Newkirk Road, Richmond Hill, Ontario, Canada
L4C 3G5

Scholastic Inc.
730 Broadway, New York, NY 10003, USA

Ashton Scholastic Limited
Private Bag 1, Penrose, Auckland, New Zealand

Ashton Scholastic Pty Limited
PO Box 579, Gosford, NSW 2250, Australia

Scholastic Publications Ltd.
Villiers House , Clarendon Avenue, Leamington Spa,
Warwickshire, CV32 5PR, UK

Author's note: Although the characters are fictional, to the best of my knowledge the historical facts in this book are true.

Canadian Cataloguing in Publication Data

Woodbury, Mary, 1935-
    Letting go

ISBN 0-590-74047-4

I. Title.

PS8595.063L4 1992   jC813'.54   C91-094233-1
PZ7.W66Le 1992

6 5 4 3 2 1   Printed in Canada   2 3 4 5 6/9
             Manufactured by Gagné Printing Ltd.

To Mary MacAllister Darby
my grandmother
1867 - 1945

and Grace Darby Harker
my mother
1901 - 1985

1

Grasping the polished wooden railing in both hands, Sara did a little dance, right there on the front deck of the ferry. The other passengers were still filing on, and wouldn't notice her. Besides, she was excited enough not to care if they did. It was the Victoria Day long weekend, 1956, and Sara Jane Collins was heading out to Toronto's Centre Island all by herself, to spend the next three months with her grandma. After school finished in four weeks, her summer buddy, Billy Best, would arrive with his grandma and his dad.

Sara's grandma Maggie Shaw collected people like some folk collect stamps. She rented out rooms in her huge Island house, to both friends and relatives — a group she affectionately called "the menagerie." Sara was glad that this time, by going out a whole month before school ended, she would have her grandma mostly to herself, at least for a while.

Sara needed to have someone to herself. Her mom had a new baby to look after — John Paul, the afterthought — and her dad was always busy studying or teaching. Apart from that, Sara wanted to spend time alone with her grandmother because Maggie had been sick, really sick. Sara was worried about her.

She raced up the iron steps of the ferry and dashed the length of the top deck to the prow. Shielding her eyes from the glare of the sun on the waves, she strained to see if her grandma was waiting on the Centre Island docks. But the Island was too far away. The distant green shoreline blurred and Sara blinked from the effort of staring. The cluster of small islands — Ward's, Algonquin, Centre, and Hanlan's Point — stretched across the horizon.

She leaned close to the railing, tracing her name over and over with one finger, wishing she had a pencil or a pen to dint the wood, to leave a mark. One that everyone could see and know she had stood here.

Blaat! The noise of the ship's horn made her jump. The warning whistle shrieked. The great gangplank rumbled and clunked shut. The *Trillium,* the biggest Toronto Harbour ferry, churned its way into the open water. Deep green waves sloshed against the sides of the boat. Lake

2

breezes lifted Sara's black curls and tossed them around her oval face.

Her skin was still pale from the long winter. Her blue-flecked hazel eyes, framed by long lashes that stuck to her cheeks if she slept too deeply, stared out over the water. Sara wasn't fat, just sturdy, with long legs and arms, slim hands, bony fingers and big feet.

She rested her middle against the railing and bent outwards to let the breeze flow over her arms and face. Turning to glimpse the Toronto skyline as it receded, she was startled to catch the eye of a white gull flying by, its powerful wings spread wide to ride the currents. That's what her science teacher had said they did — rode the currents to save their strength.

Sara's arms tingled. How she wished she could fly with the birds, speeding away from the noise of the city. Soaring high, diving low, free to glide. Gulls didn't have music lessons to go to, rules and regulations to follow, chores and errands to run, classes to attend. Sara giggled, picturing a flock of gulls waddling down the school corridor. The caretaker sure wouldn't like that. He'd have to clean up the bird-do.

Sara turned her back on the scudding sailboats, the green waves. Maybe she should go below and hang over the brass railing that enclosed the throbbing engines, watch the giant knuckles of steel lift and fall, first one arm and then the other, propelling the old ferry across the stretch of lake water as smoothly and calmly as John Paul's rocking cradle. She strolled toward the staircase.

"Getting an early start on summer, Sara Jane?" Kevin the deck-hand called from the bottom of the steps, his elbows leaning on the bannister. The two had known each other for a few years now, ever since Kevin started working on the ferries. "Is that your bike chained to the front? It's awful big."

Sara pulled herself up to her full height. "Maggie bought it for me."

"Too bad about her heart. Is she okay?"

Sara stared at Kevin hard. His brush cut, partly grown out, made him look like a thug. "I'm going to keep an eye on her." Her voice loud.

"My dad died of a heart attack." Kevin rubbed the back of his neck.

"Maggie's okay. She's got to take it easy, the doctor said, so she doesn't have another heart attack. Another one could be . . . " Sara's face flushed. She wanted to run.

"Fatal." Kevin finished the sentence for her. But Sara was pushing her way through the crowded, stuffy inner cabin. She wanted to see the engine so badly she could taste the heat and oil on her tongue. She wanted the steamy throbbing to fill her ears, to drown out Kevin's voice and her own thoughts.

4

Kevin caught up to her just as she reached the solid metal door to the engine room.

"Look, kid, I'm sorry. Here, do you want some milk?" He unscrewed the cap of his blue Thermos and offered the bottle to her. Sara shook her head.

"I've always had a big mouth. You say Maggie's okay. Some heart attack victims survive for years. My dad smoked and drank too much."

The *Trillium*'s steady rhythm changed. The grand old ferry's engine slowed as she turned towards the Centre Island docks. It was too late for Sara to see the paddlewheel in action. Maybe next time.

"Did you hear the latest dockyard gossip?" Kevin wiped a drop of milk from his chin, screwed the cap back on his Thermos and shrugged his shoulders. "Metro Toronto is retiring the *Trillium*. Says she's too old, needs repairs, and there aren't enough passengers. I'll be stuck on the smaller diesel ferries. It's a shame, I've gotten kinda attached to the old bucket. She gives a smooth ride."

Sara followed Kevin as he headed to the front deck. "What will they do with her?"

"They turned the *Bluebell* into a garbage scow." Kevin reached the accordion gate at the front of the ferry. The crowd collecting made a path for Sara as she fought her way through to stand beside him.

"What will they do with the *Trillium?*" Sara asked again, her hand on his sleeve.

"Take off this superstructure and use the old hull." He stopped. "Look, I'm not even sure, kid, nothing's for sure, it's only gossip. They used to haul the old ferries out into the middle of the harbour and set them ablaze." He hurried out to the gangplank, locking the gate behind him.

A fat man with a red face spoke up. "The whole city came down and watched the *John Hanlan* burn. They clapped and cheered. I was there. It was some fire."

"What a way to go," a tall woman carrying a bag full of books said. Horn-rimmed glasses hung on a string around her neck. "Stinking of rubbish or sinking in flames. Take your pick."

Thump! The ferry thudded against the ugly brown sacks draped around the Island dock. The *Trillium* shuddered and stopped. Captain Joe, Kevin and the other deck-hand uncoiled ropes, leapt to the pulleys. Seagulls rose from unpainted pilings, scolding the sailors and the crowd with high-pitched cries. Sara couldn't spot the pure white one that had flown beside her when she had been on the top deck. Was it there? Was it screaming, too?

"Sara, Sara, I'm over here." It was Maggie, waving frantically. She stood behind the white picket barricade, a stocky woman with white hair sticking out in waves, round cheeks, round glasses, dimples and a cleft in her chin. Her face shone tanned and wrinkly in the morning sunlight. She was wearing a loose blue paisley cotton dress. Next to the other waiting people, Maggie looked short, really short. Was she shrinking?

Sara grabbed her bike and rolled it down the gangplank. The wooden slats went thunk, thunk, thunk as she wheeled it across the dock to her grandmother's side.

"You're some big, you are." Maggie reached across the handlebars and gave Sara a big hug. A whiff of Lily of the Valley cologne filled the air. Maggie's cheek against Sara's felt softer than the baby John Paul's.

"You just saw me a week ago, Maggie," Sara laughed. "I haven't grown that much."

"Being out here changes my point of view. Changes everything." Maggie rescued her old bike from the rack. "I'm glad you've come, lassie."

The *Trillium* tooted its horn. Stragglers with shopping bags, strollers and bikes hurried on board for the trip back to the city.

"The bike's okay?" Maggie watched as Sara swung her leg over the seat. Her eyes sparkled. "Your mother said I was spoiling you when I bought you that. But I figured I can spoil my youngest granddaughter if I want. Besides, if you expect to keep up with me you'll need it." She climbed on her bike and pedalled off down the cinder track.

Sara rolled down the pathway after her. The cinders crunched under the wheels. She sang to herself, "On the Island, I'm on the Island. I've got the whole summer ahead of me. No more music lessons, Girl Guides, Sunday school. Just commuting to class for four weeks and then vacation."

"The ice cream store opened yesterday," Maggie shouted across the walkway. Her front wheel squeaked.

Sara licked her lips and started pedalling faster. Maggie's wheel squeaked louder.

"I better fix that for you when we get home. After we've had ice cream."

"You can fix that, my girl, but there's some things that won't be mended so easy." Maggie sighed. "Wait till you see. Wait till you see what's been going on. Or rather, what's been coming down."

2

Two angry crows cawed by the side of the path and flew away. Sara and Maggie pedaled slowly across the wide expanse of grass and black cinder. Sara glanced over at her grandmother.

"What's coming down? You said something was coming down."

"You'll see when we get to the bridge."

They cycled past the old carousel, its roof slanty and its sides boarded up. When Sara had been a little kid she'd ridden that merry-go-round time and time again. Two rides for a nickel. She would have stayed all day if she'd had enough money or her mom had let her. She had been frightened at first, especially by the big horses on the outside edge that went up and down so fast. She'd ridden on Daddy's knee on the ponies that didn't move. Finally she'd grown brave enough to ride the big horses. Her favourite had been a pure white one with a blonde mane and tail.

She remembered one day, one day in particular, riding her horse, holding her ticket in her hand, the only kid on the merry-go-round. Her mother waited by the gate. Every time the merry-go-round went past, Sara waved. Her mother stood, arms folded across her chest. When the music stopped, Sara had pleaded for another turn.

"No." Her mother had grasped her hand firmly. Sara tugged and tugged, pulling away from her mother and running across the green meadow.

"Come back, Sara!" her mother had shouted. Next thing Sara knew, she was being held tight, her hand squeezed, her feet dragging, as her mother hauled her down the path back to Maggie's house. The rest of the scene disappeared in a painful fog.

Sara's breath came fast. She pedalled faster.

"Who's chasing you?" Maggie called.

Sara slowed, waiting for her grandma's steady cycling to bring her closer. "Nobody."

"Come on, what's up?" Maggie's glasses glinted in the sun.

Sara took a deep breath and shivered. "Kevin says the *Trillium*'s going to be a garbage scow."

"I know. Captain Joe's some upset. He became a ferryboat captain 'cause he rode on her when he was a wee laddie. I've always liked her the best, she gives a smooth ride."

"It's not fair."

Maggie looked away suddenly, her eyes scanning the trees, the fields, the distant canals with the luxury cruisers lining the banks.

Sara didn't know whether to ride on or to slow down and talk. She had come out here to get away from everything, and it looked like she had just traded problems the way her friend Billy Best traded comics.

"Love is a many splendoured thing," the loudspeakers blared from Manitou Street. They had reached the concrete bridge. Maggie led the way, walking her bike, whistling along with the music. Sara leaned her new Raleigh against the freshly painted green bench and followed Maggie to the ice cream stand.

"Maple walnut!" Maggie propped her wrinkled elbows on the counter.

The owner already had his scoop dipped in Maggie's favourite flavour. "I suppose you want chocolate ripple, Sara Jane." Then he jammed great gooey swirls of the cold sweet stuff into a fat sugar cone. Sara licked her lips.

"Tall as your grandma, I see." He handed her the cone. "Remember when you couldn't see over the counter? Time marches on."

"Good to the last drop." Maggie shoved the ice cream down into the cone with her tongue, the way she used to with Sara's when Sara was small so the little girl wouldn't drop her scoop onto the sidewalk instead of into her tummy. Sara felt like laughing, watching Maggie, listening to the music, hearing the same old talk from the dairy man. It was homey.

"Pity about the *Trillium*, eh! She sure gives a smooth ride." The man wiped his big hands on his starched white apron, leaving a streak of chocolate across the wide expanse. "Captain Joe will be lost without her. I suppose in the long run they'll shut me down, too."

Maggie and Sara strolled the length of the main drag, pushing their bikes with their right hands, balancing cones in their left. The smell of piping hot french fries made Sara wish she hadn't eaten at home. But her mom had made pancakes for her send-off. After breakfast, her dad had given her a big hug, grabbed his library books and sprinted for the door.

"Be good, Sara. I'll see you when you come home to visit. When I come back from summer school in Montreal, I'll take you fishing." He stooped to get out the door, he was so tall. Then he was gone.

Her mom had driven her to the docks, talked to Captain Joe about delivering her suitcase to Maggie's, and given Sara her marching orders.

"Keep an eye on Maggie. Don't let her do any heavy work. Remember she's a lot more fragile than she thinks she is. See you next week. I'll phone every day or so. Be good." Her mother's hug was brisk. The starch in her blouse smelled lemony.

"You're pretty quiet, my girl." Maggie threw the tip of her cone to a cluster of sparrows.

Sara tossed her cone tip, too. The little birds gathered round, pecking happily.

Could she say that coming out to the Island this year seemed like a much longer trip, not just a jaunt across the harbour, that she felt something momentous was going on?

She looked out over the lakeshore. A sea of sand, clean and raked, stretched out to the blue-green shoreline. Waves were crashing over the breakwater. The sky to the east was filled with dark clouds. A storm brewed.

But she shouldn't be able to see the lakeshore from here! Sara felt blood rush to her head. Where was the big hotel that had always blocked the view? Smack in the middle of the vacant lot at the end of the main drag stood a giant yellow bulldozer.

"I was afraid you wouldn't want to come if I told you," Maggie whispered, her hand on Sara's arm. "Metro Council has decided to turn the whole of the Island into a park. Sixty-five houses on Centre have been knocked down and burnt. The theatre's closed."

"Where's the hotel, the big hotel?" Sara muttered, afraid of the storm gathering inside her chest.

"They took two days to destroy it. I still see it in my mind's eye — all that spotless white clapboard, the wide porches, the swanky tourists, lawns like carpets. It can happen so fast."

Sara picked up a jagged stone from the pavement and threw it hard at the bulldozer.

"Machines just do what they're told, Sara. It's the gaps that bother me — where houses used to be, where friends used to be . . . " Maggie reached across the boardwalk. Her hand in Sara's was small, tanned and speckled. "Och, let's go home, *mo ghaoil*."

3

Maggie's great rambling three-storey house on Hiawatha Street stood back from the sidewalk, its green siding as dark as the fresh-mowed lawn. A wide wooden fire escape wove its way down the left side from the attic to the second floor roof, past Sara's porch to the ground. Counting balconies and alcoves, there were eighteen rooms. Like Anne of Green Gables' house, thought Sara, but she sure was no orphan and Maggie wasn't stern like the old lady in the book.

Bright yellow forsythia and purple lilacs bloomed close to the screened porch. A forgotten croquet hoop leaned by the cedar hedge.

"Come on, slowpoke." Maggie opened the front door. "You tak' the high road and I'll tak' the low road, and I'll be in Scotland afore you," she sang.

Sara wheeled her bike to the wooden stand

by the back door. An old-fashioned washing machine, more like a barrel with legs, stood on the back stoop. Maggie appeared behind the screen door. "I've washed all the bedding. You can help me fix up the rooms. Captain Joe's coming back to stay this weekend, and your cousin Arthur's due in a week. Right now he's learning how to be a summer city park gardener, off in Niagara Falls."

The neighbour's dog let out a howl.

"Shut up, Nero," Sara shouted.

"*Thrushima*!" Maggie added.

"What?" Sara followed her grandmother into the kitchen.

"It's Gaelic for 'get lost' or 'beat it'."

"I always wondered. Is that all you remember?"

"Not much call for the Gaelic in Toronto, *mo ghaoil*." Maggie spent most of the year in her house in the city, moving out to the Island only in the summers. Her Toronto house was right next door to Sara's. In fact their two houses — the Collins' and Maggie's — were joined on one side, or "semi-detached," as the real estate agents say. "It's a long way from the Isle of Arran to Canada, that's for sure. I'll never go back now. I'll content myself with this wee island and the short journey out and back across the harbour. Lake Ontario is no ocean but it's the best I can ask for. Enough of this palaver, chickadee. Put on the kettle."

The pipes groaned as Sara turned on the tap.

"You'll have to turn on the burner, lamb." Maggie set out the Blue Willow cups. She scraped a stray crumb off the new checkered oilcloth. "So I have to keep an eye on you for another year?"

"Don't forget, I'm keeping an eye on you too." The two of them leaned across the table, staring into each other's eyes — until they giggled and their eyes crossed. Sara had to break first.

She filled the teapot with hot water, poured it out and put in three teaspoons of loose tea, filling the brown pot to the brim with boiling water.

"Ethel gave you strict orders, did she?" Maggie's eyes shone bright blue, as blue as her china cups. She took a spoon and stirred the tea water to speed the steeping. "Don't go away, I'll be right back." Maggie scurried down the hall to the bathroom.

Sara twirled her cup in its saucer, watching the blue trees, the wooden bridge, the stooped figures in the Blue Willow pattern spin like the old merry-go-round.

She was thinking about the previous Saturday, when, as usual, she, her mom and Maggie had bargain hunted in Eaton's basement in Toronto, then gone to the Georgian Room for lunch.

But that last Saturday had been different.

First the waitress asked whether Sara wasn't too old for the kiddie menu. Then her mom noticed Sara's dirty nails and sent her to wash. Finally, to make matters worse, her mom and Maggie had a fight.

Sara was coming back from the bathroom, threading her way among the tables. Even halfway across the room she could hear her mom's voice.

"Mother, sell the Island house while you can. It's too much for you."

"The menagerie counts on me, Ethel Collins. They need me. Where would they stay if I closed down?" Maggie's eyebrows bristled. "I love the Island."

Sara slipped into her chair. Her mother grabbed her hand and checked the fingers. They were spotless. "Eat your lunch before it gets cold," she ordered and turned back to Maggie.

"Mother, you've got to take it easy. The doctor says — "

"I know what the doctor says." Maggie's jaw was clenched so tight the cleft in her chin had disappeared.

"I'm not coming out to help. John Paul's too tiny and with Fred off in Montreal, someone's got to mind the house, and your house, too. Besides . . . " Sara's mother's face had furrows right across the forehead. "I worry."

"You're good at that, Ethel," Maggie said.

The air around the table seemed charged with electricity. Sara sat with her fork in her hand, feeling funny all the way to her toes.

"Sit up straight, Sara. You look like the hunchback of Notre Dame." Sara straightened her back so fast it cracked.

"It's not Sara's fault, Ethel, leave her out of it." Maggie bit her lip. "I'm opening the Island house next weekend." She clamped her mouth shut.

Suddenly, dizzy and all, Sara had an idea.

"I could go with Grandma," she sputtered. "I could keep an eye on her."

Her mother's steel-blue eyes drilled into her. "What good would that do? What if something happened to her?"

Maggie's face relaxed. "Sara would be a lot of help, Ethel. She's a big girl. Thirteen is some big, isn't it? And if something's going to happen to me, it will happen."

Ethel Collins sat folding and refolding her linen napkin. Maggie and Sara went back to cleaning their plates. They didn't dare look at each other.

"What about school?"

"I could commute like the kids from Ward's Island do." Sara felt breathless. "I could come home for lunch every day. Give you reports."

Above them the huge chandeliers gleamed. The room was filled with piano music, the clatter of dishes, the swish of passing waitresses carrying overloaded trays. The smell of hot food wafted from under the funny little silver hats that covered the plates. Sara felt like the whole of the Georgian Room was waiting for her mother's reply.

"Maybe. I'll have to think about it. Sara's still a child."

"The right age to send away for the summer. I could teach her to cook."

Her mother stood behind Sara's chair, pulling on her worn black coat, her mended gloves. "I don't want Sara given in to. I don't want you being soft with her."

Maggie, wiping her lips, tucking her lace hankie up her sleeve, rested her gaze on Sara's face for a moment. "She'll be too busy to get into trouble." She winked.

For a minute or so they stood there, the three of them, Sara's mother solid and imposing in plain black, her back stiff, her shoulders firm; Maggie, stooped and stocky in her rumpled flowered dress; and Sara between them. Sara had felt pulled both ways, wanting to go with her grandmother, wanting the Island, and at the same time wanting to stay with her mother in the semi on Dufferin with its polished floors and striped wallpaper and shiny-leaved rubber plant and her friend Susan down the street.

"All right! She can go, but if there's any

nonsense she will have to come back." Ethel Collins looked grim.

And here she was. Sara poured herself a cup of steaming tea and dropped a teaspoon of sugar into it.

"So did your mother give you any pointers on watching me?" Maggie walked back into the kitchen, cleaning her glasses with a tissue.

"Mom just said I wasn't to let you overdo it."

"Well, that sounds reasonable. But I'm not sitting around all the time. We've got work to do and rummy to play, and songs to sing, and stories to tell." Maggie stirred her tea. "We'll have a fine time, the two of us."

"Mom says I'm like you."

"Shaw women are all pretty feisty, she should talk. But I'm not giving in to this heart trouble business."

"She says you're as stubborn as Cassiopea. Who's Cassiopea?"

"A constellation in the night sky. Named after the Celtic goddess Cassiopea. You can see her throne right across from the big dipper. I'll show you tonight if you like."

"After we play rummy?" Sara cleared away the cups.

Maggie handed her a pile of sheets and towels. "First, make the beds."

"Tote that barge, lift that bale, I know! " Sara laughed as she headed for the stairway.

"You show promise, *mo ghaoil.*" Maggie put down a pail and mop and came to the bottom of the steps, throwing her arms around Sara in a quick hug.

Sara felt warm as she skipped up the stairs two at a time, the pile of laundry nearly tumbling from her arms.

* * *

By the time Sara fell into bed that night she had helped clean the whole house. Her knees hurt, her shoulders ached. For supper Maggie had made chicken and dumplings that were so delicious Sara had eaten until she was stuffed.

Lying between the cool fresh sheets, Sara watched Cassiopea through the window. She propped her head on folded arms and stretched her sore body all the way down to her toes. Her feet were definitely further down the bed than last year.

She wondered how tall Billy was now. When she had seen him at Christmas he had grown heaps. Maybe he'd be too old to play with? But then he'd gotten a new hockey game for his birthday, so he must still like playing.

Every year she and Billy walked the length of the large rocks that made up the breakwater. They always slipped somewhere and got soaked, toppling into the cold waves on the deep side or slipping into the calm shallow side near the shore. This year she wanted to walk the whole thing without falling in. It would be harder than walking the balance beam in gym, but she could do that easily now, she had good balance.

Outside, the birds stopped singing. The low sound of water lapping on the beach, the whisper of leaves in the trees lulled Sara to sleep.

4

Sara woke early, wondering where she was. Opening her eyes, she spotted the pink pansies on the wallpaper, the damp spot in the corner where the roof leaked and the sun streaming in the dozens of small windowpanes. Her room was really the porch on the second floor. It was like sleeping outdoors. A drunken bluebottle banged against the screen.

In the semi on Dufferin her room was dark. One small light bulb hung from the middle of the high ceiling. Traffic roared down the street outside, day and night. Outside, you had to watch for speeding cars, thieves and bad guys. It was hard to feel safe, as Sara had always felt here, in her screened and windowed porch. No cars, no traffic, only birds and squirrels. And no people to worry about — unless you counted the grouchy neighbour who didn't like kids, Mr. Quantz.

She threw open a window to let in the fresh air from the lake. She inhaled a deep breath of dew and lilac, mixed with the smell of lake water.

Across the back yards she could spot the black squirrels scampering, and robins hopping. The grouchy neighbour's black dog sat chained to the old man's back porch. Past his house lay a huge pile of charred wooden beams where Peabody's house used to be. Sara sighed all the way to her bones.

The third step creaked as she tiptoed down the stairs. How did Billy Best's favourite joke go? What did one dummy say to the other? Wear your rubber boots when you climb the stairs — there's a *creek* on the third step. Boy, was she looking forward to Billy coming, and to seeing his grandmother, Granny Pitts.

Sara took herself on a tour of the house. Yesterday she'd been too busy cleaning it to see it properly. Even empty, it felt full of life. There was cousin Arthur's wicker chair where he sat to read. Maggie's multicolored afghan lay folded on the back of the horsehair couch with its sagging middle. A clutter of books and photo albums covered the dining room table, and sheet music was propped up on the organ. Figurines and knick-knacks decorated every shelf and table.

Sara straightened the Blue Boy picture hanging in the hall. Her long thin fingers patted dresser scarves, picked lint off worn carpets. The ancient refrigerator with its motor throbbing on top, coiled like a spring, broke into a loud hum as she walked past to the back of the house. She went up two steps to the apartment where gloomy Gladys Waterby lived in the summer. Gladys wouldn't be arriving for over a month.

The door swung open. The smell of stale tobacco smoke hit Sara. She expected to see Gladys, cigarette between her fingers — bony, beak-nosed Gladys, with her feathery hair as black as a raven's.

Sara's cousin Arthur, when he was there, lived in the attic. "Arthur, under the eaves. Our naturalist, up in the air with the birds," Maggie joked about her grandson. Arthur, who was an ancient 22, had a girlfriend named Alice, an artist who lived on nearby Ward's Island.

Captain Joe's room smelled of old socks and pipe smoke. Sara ran down the front steps towards the suite where the Bests stayed. Billy's baseball glove and bat leaned inside the door.

Then she heard milk bottles clanging in the old fridge. Footsteps sounded in the kitchen. Water ran through the pipes. Maggie was whistling "You tak' the High Road." Sara dashed to her room to pull on some clothes — corduroy slacks and a longsleeved red shirt. She hunted through her suitcase for matching socks.

"Come on, lazybones." Maggie's voice rang up the staircase.

"Coming, grandma."

Sara wolfed down a bowl of oatmeal with brown sugar and cream, then three pieces of toast with grape jelly. She strained the last of her tea through her teeth, leaving the tea-leaves on the inside of the cup. Then she turned the cup upside down on the saucer, twirled it three times and made a wish.

"Tell my fortune," she pleaded. "Please, Maggie."

"Such foolishness." Maggie grinned and took the Blue Willow cup from her.

"I know. But it's fun and sometimes it works." Sara's eyes sparkled. This was like old times.

Maggie's glasses slid down her nose. She pushed them up. "I see a tall fair friend coming soon."

"That's Billy."

"I see a cluster of leaves — near the bottom."

"That's the rest of the menagerie." Sara slapped her knee. "You're right on today. What else do you see?"

"Looks like a house off to the side." Maggie put the cup down.

"That's our house, I bet. With Mom, Dad and the baby." Sara picked up the cup and stared at the tea-leaves. "Do you think I could learn how?"

Maggie ran water into the dishpan. "I don't

27

want you making too much of it. Us Celts don't like to get carried away with our powers, lassie. 'Twouldn't do at all."

"I won't make too much of it. I promise."

Maggie scratched her chin where a tiny white hair was sprouting. "Make a fresh pot."

The two of them hunkered over the table.

"After the body gives you the cup, take a deep breath, clear your mind of everything else, look deep into their eyes, touch their hand if possible. Then look into the cup. Don't say anything right away. Give it time to speak. Leastways, that's the way I've always done it. Sometimes nothing happens. Depends on what mood the reader is in, what kind of a body is asking."

"Let me try." Sara jiggled up and down in her chair.

Maggie took a last swallow of tea, turned her cup upside down and twirled it three times for good luck. "Now, *mo ghaoil*."

Sara blinked fiercely. Her mouth felt dry. Taking her grandmother's Blue Willow cup in both hands she paused, looked deep into Maggie's eyes, but not too long because she didn't want to giggle. She patted the back of Maggie's hand, feeling the skin soft and thin like tissue paper.

"I see an island in your future. Look, right there. And a boat with a sail. There's a crowd of people waving, their arms are raised."

Maggie shuddered and grabbed the cup. "Here, let me see that. Is the boat sailing to the west or to the east? It's got a sail, you say? Am I alone?" Her hand shook as she lifted the cup closer. The tea-leaves dropped to the bottom. "Och, aye, it's gone. It's gone."

Sara put her hand on Maggie's shoulder. The old woman's face was white. "Are you okay?"

Maggie shook her head, pulled her arms in to her sides. She began mumbling to herself. "If it's a sailboat going west — but that's only an old tale from the Celts — and we're in Canada." She shook her head. "You've got to promise . . . "

"What?" Sara asked. What was her grandma talking about?

"You've got to promise to take it with a grain of salt." Maggie pushed her chair away from the table and walked to the sink, ran water into the dishpan and added soap, thrust her hands into the hot water. "Life needs a little mystery. It needs a good dose of common sense as well."

Sara wiped the cups and put them in the cupboard. The clock ticked in the silent, cluttered kitchen.

Maggie let the water out, the drain gurgling like a giant's cough. Without saying a word, she went into the dark hallway, flipped on the light and opened the tiny door to the closet under the stairs. She hauled out a battered leather suitcase.

"Let me lift that!" Sara dropped the tea-towel on the kitchen table and ran to Maggie. She shoved her grandma aside and pulled the heavy case into the living room.

"Over there beside the sewing machine." Maggie straightened, closed the small door, turned off the hall light.

Sara recognized the suitcase. It was filled with remnants of material, old ties, clean old stockings, leftovers of fabric. She snapped open the lid. Pieces of brightly coloured cloth tumbled out like kids into a playground.

"What are you going to make? Can I help?"

"A rug, a good old-fashioned rag rug. You can help choose the bits."

Sara sat back on her heels. Maggie moved the figurines off the old treadle sewing machine and lifted the lid. "It will give me something to do while you're off at school every day. Now run along."

"What about picking the bits?"

"Tonight, lamb, after supper. Making a rug's a long project. It will take all summer." She sighed, pulled the leather ottoman over and sat before the open suitcase, her eyes sparkling like those of a prince sitting in front of a box of jewels. "Nothing like a good dose of common sense when the mystery gets too much for a body," she whispered, talking to herself as Sara left the room. Sara couldn't for the life of her figure out what her grandma was talking about.

* * *

Down on the shore, the waves crashed against the breakwater. The beach was empty.

Sara bent, chose a flat pebble and flung it carefully along the top of the waves. It skipped four times.

She had read Maggie's cup, she had looked into the tea-leaves and let her imagination go just where it wanted, and she had seen a boat with Maggie in it. But of course her grandmother was right, it was only a game, you shouldn't take it too seriously. But then why had Maggie grabbed the cup?

A foghorn sounded. She flung another stone. It bounced three times and sank beneath the waves.

Sara dropped onto the warm beach and began pulling sand into a big mound. When she was finished, she stuck a twig on the top, and looked around for a flag. A dirty cast-off ribbon lay by a bench. She dusted it off and tied it to the twig. There's Sara, Sara on top of the hill. She glanced along the beach — all she could see was an old man and his dog off in the distance. She yanked off her running shoes and socks, and danced around her castle. She danced and leapt until she got dizzy, fell down and lay there, watching the trees spin round above her.

5

Sara was glad when the last day of school finally arrived. She'd miss the daily ferry ride to and from the Island, but she sure wouldn't miss all the schoolwork.

At noon she grabbed her report, waved good-bye to her friend Susan, and hurried home to her parents' house for lunch. The sound of piano music drifted down the block. Her mother was playing marches on Maggie's piano, so Sara marched up the steps. She glanced at Maggie's half of the semi with its trailing ivy, geranium pots, the porch crowded with old wicker chairs and an ancient sofa. Her own house had a fresh coat of grey paint, and one pot of flowers and two aluminum folding chairs on the porch. "Is that you, Sara?" The music had stopped. Her mother came out from behind the screen door. She was dressed in a plain navy blue dress with a single strand of beads and matching blue earrings. Her hair was pulled back and neatly rolled in a bun. "Your dad will be home any minute. Lunch is ready." She locked Maggie's door and walked across to the Collins' side.

Sara handed her report card to her mother with a grin. She'd snagged a look on the way down the street. It was fine — all A's except for a B in science. She hung up her sweater in the closet. The house seemed very still. John Paul must be napping.

"I put the baby down early so we could have a little visit before you go back to Maggie and your dad leaves for Montreal."

Sara followed her mother into the kitchen where the table was set with a crisp green cloth, napkins in little holders, a vase of fresh flowers. Beside her plate was a wrapped gift.

"It's not a bicycle, but it's a little graduation present." Her mother's voice was low.

Her dad came bounding through the door, ducking carefully to clear the beam. "How's tricks?" He gave Sara a big hug, lifting her up high enough so his fuzzy cheek scratched hers. He kissed her mother's cheek, too.

Sara's mother handed him the report card. Sara unwrapped her gift, folding the paper so it could be used again. Inside was a bird book with bright, coloured photographs and drawings. She leaned across and pecked her mom's and then her dad's cheek. "Thanks."

"Looks good." Sara's dad propped the card up in the middle of the table. "I wish I didn't have to go to school this summer. I'd rather knock about with this smart kid. We've got a date to go fishing, right, when I get back?"

"We can't always do what we want." Sara's mother handed around the plates. Hot chili con carne, brown toast and a little coleslaw.

"Cheer up, Ethel. We'll be back home before you know it, Sara and me. Where else can we get a spread like this?"

The baby started to cry. Sara's mother wiped her hands on her apron and stood quickly.

"Leave him for a minute, Ethel, he'll be fine. I've got some news." Fred Collins reached into his jacket pocket and pulled out an envelope. He passed it across the table to his wife, turned and winked at Sara.

"I've been offered a vice-principalship in September. A raise in pay goes with it. Your mother's a miracle worker, stretching my salary all the way around the four of us. Come next fall she'll have more to manage with. And with any kind of luck, I'll be home more."

Ethel Collins was staring at the paper in her hands, reading it again. "Well, at least that's one worry off my plate."

"You worry too much, Ethel." Mr. Collins got up to make the tea.

"Someone has to worry." Sara's mother took one more mouthful of chili and ran up the stairs to rescue the crying baby.

"Finish your lunch, Sara, and I'll drive you to the ferry. How are things out there?"

Sara told him about the hotel being torn down, and the hole where Peabody's house used to be, and Maggie's rug. "She needs more strips. She's gathering bits from everyone. She's hung on to lots of scraps — stuff from the California aunts, Arthur's dad's air force tie . . . "

Her dad pulled out his hankie and passed it over, then went to take off his tie.

"Old ones, silly."

"We'll rummage through the closet. There's some real ugly ties hanging in there," her dad said, laughing.

* * *

"Don't get too near the currant bushes," Sara warned her cousin Arthur as they put up the croquet set, back on the Island. "There's wasps and old Mr. Quantz to worry about, and I don't know whose bite is worse." The currant bushes belonged to the grouchy neighbour who didn't like kids.

The big day was here. The rest of the menagerie, minus Gladys Waterby, who wouldn't be coming for two more days, was due to arrive any minute. The whistle of the departing ferry had faded on the air.

Sara straightened the hoops and bent down to tie orange surveyor's tape to each one.

"What a bum view!" It was Billy, shouting from the end of the block. Sara jumped up, pulling her shorts over her hind end. Trust Billy to catch her with her pants down.

"Mind your own bee's knees, you skinny creep," she hollered back. She wanted to race down the block and give him a big hug — but that would look stupid and besides, his dad was with him. Billy was hauling suitcases in his old red wagon with the slats on the sides. His dad was wheeling a bike.

"Where's Granny Pitts?" Arthur peered from under his bushy eyebrows that grew together in a thick line across his forehead. He reached for one of the suitcases and headed for the screen door.

"She stopped for tea on the main drag. The place sure looks different with all the houses gone. Do you think this is our last summer?" Mr. Best asked as he followed Arthur into the house.

Billy was still outside. "Hi, kid," he said, drawing up beside Sara.

"Hi." Sara lifted her head to stare up at him. He must have grown a lot since Christmas. His blonde brushcut nearly touched the top of the door frame. But his crooked smile was the same as ever as he stood grinning, waiting for her to say something.

"I got a new bike."

"I'll race you after lunch." His voice cracked on lunch.

"Time to eat," Maggie chirped from the porch. "My, Billy, you sure have sprouted."

Arthur broke in. "Going out for basketball this fall?" he said to Billy, then turned and chucked Sara under the chin. "Guess you'll have to eat more Wheaties, eh, kid? Won't be long until you have to buy those sweaters with bumps, like the older girls wear." He tugged on his straggly moustache.

Sara blushed and hurried into the kitchen. Maggie dished out tomato soup and grilled cheese sandwiches, Sara's favourite. Sara sat staring at the birds in the currant bushes outside the window.

Arthur's chair scraped as he pulled it up to the table. "Billy sure has grown. Last time I saw Granny Pitts, she looked like she was on her last legs. Another house has been torn down. It's hard to keep up with the changes."

Sara lifted a spoonful of soup to her lips. It was so hot it nearly burnt her tongue.

6

"Want help with the dishes?" Arthur stood in the hallway holding the *Globe and Mail*. He ran a hand through his tousled brown hair.

Sara shook her head as she piled the plates beside the sink and ran water into the dishpan. Now that Arthur was here she could relax a little, let him help keep an eye on Maggie, let him make sure she rested her "various veins," as Granny Pitts called them.

Arthur sauntered off to his big old wicker chair. Maggie settled on the sofa with the crossword puzzle, her head on two souvenir cushions from Niagara Falls, the crocheted afghan over her legs.

"What's a five letter word for harbinger of spring?"

"Robin," Arthur said. He stretched his long legs out into the centre of the room. Arthur was nearly as tall as Sara's dad.

By the time Sara had finished washing the sticky soup pot, Maggie's whistle-snore floated through the house. A snuffle in, a whistle out. Sara smiled at the sight of Maggie asleep on the couch. A halo of white hair framed her face, her mouth was open, the newspaper had slid off her heaving chest. Long strands of rag strips were coiled in heaps by her feet, more rag bits overflowed from a felt bag hooked to the chair. Scissors and various spools of thread were scattered on the floor.

"Is Maggie trying to make a wall-to-wall carpet?" Arthur chuckled as he retrieved the crossword and the pencil from the floor. He placed them on the end table under the Chinese-lady lamp with the parasol lampshade. "See you later, kid."

He was probably off to see Alice. All Arthur ever seemed to do was go over to his girlfriend Alice's or go to meetings about saving the Island, saving the birds, or stopping nuclear war.

Sara checked her grandma one more time. She was snoring peacefully. Sara dashed outside and flung herself on the swing with its thumb-thick ropes, hanging between two giant chestnut trees. She pumped her legs until she could see all the way down the street to the lake.

Billy bounded down the side stairs and gave her a big push from behind before he threw himself on the hammock.

"Wow! Is this good, or what? Have you read the latest romance — *Kiss and Tell* by Lucy Lips?"

Sara groaned. The toes of her running shoes brushed the branches. She waited until she was halfway to the ground then leapt off, landing solid and firm as a tree trunk, just as she did at the end of her exercise routine in gym class.

She sauntered around to the back of the house and unlocked her bike, then wheeled it around to the front. She pushed it right up beside the hammock.

Billy sprang up and grabbed it from her, pedalling off down the street like a racer. Sara stood with her hands in her pockets, grinning and bouncing on the balls of her feet.

"Neat bike!" he gasped as he pulled up to the house again, nudging the front wheel right up against her toe. "Sure gives a smooth ride."

Sara couldn't help but think of the *Trillium*. As the two friends climbed on their bikes and headed to the lakefront, Sara told Billy about the old ferry being docked, maybe forever.

The sun beat down as they flew along the wide strip of pavement that ran between the lakeshore houses and the beach. Heat haze hung over the sand. Old women and men watched sand-covered children building castles and wading pools. No one was in the water, it was far too cold. Gulls screeched, diving for fish. A musty smell lingered from yesterday's rain.

Sara and Billy rode in the direction of Hanlan's Point. When they reached the boardwalk, their tires clunked as they struggled to avoid the gaps between the wide planks. Billy pulled alongside Sara, his face glistening with sweat. "How's school?"

"I won a prize for art, and I'm on the gymnastics team. We get to go to competitions next year. Maybe on a plane."

"I rode on a plane this year. Dad took Granny and me with him to Los Angeles, on a buying trip. Department store buyers get to travel all over. But I miss him when he's gone . . ." Billy sighed. "It's bad enough having no mom." Billy's mother had died when he was born, so his grandma, Mrs. Pitts, had moved in to take care of him.

Billy continued, "We toured the movie studios in California. Boy, you should see the highways, they're like roller coasters, up and down and over. We got lost three times."

Just then three teenage girls in bikinis strutted by, giggling. One of them whistled at Billy. He nearly fell off his bike, craning his neck to watch them walk away.

"Drip." Sara leaned across and tugged on his handlebars.

"Who's your boyfriend, or is that a secret?" Billy laughed.

Sara raced off quickly with Billy in hot pursuit. They whipped past the Island school and the playground.

"I beat," Sara shouted, startling a flock of schoolyard pigeons.

"So you got a baby brother. I thought your mom looked fat at Christmas," Billy hollered into the wind from the lake. Along this stretch there wasn't any breakwater and the full force of the waves pounded onto the rocky shore.

"Babies take a lot of time. He cries a lot. At first I thought it might be okay, kind of like having a doll, but I never much liked dolls. I'd rather play dodge ball, or baseball or tag."

"So you don't like the baby?"

"I didn't say that." Sara didn't know how she felt about John Paul. He was just there all the time, needing food, needing quiet, needing changing.

"You've just got your nose out of joint, being an only child for so long."

Sara's eyes burned. "Who told you that? What makes you say that? What do you know about it anyway, you're an only kid, you don't even have a mother, she died."

Billy braked as they came to a little bridge. He climbed off his bike and leaned over the railing. The water in the lagoon flowing under them was dark green edged by muddy banks. A muskrat ducked for shelter.

Sara dropped her bike against the railing and joined him. A motorboat roared along the channel sending up a wash. Smaller and smaller waves slapped the shore.

"Sorry," she mumbled.

"It's okay. Granny Pitts and Dad were just talking, you know, the way they talk. She was calling it a 'strategy', and Dad said it wasn't a tragedy, that a baby was okay, even if the parents are older, even when folks didn't have much money." Billy pulled up a handful of grass, put two pieces together and blew. The whistle pierced the air.

A chorus of frogs croaked. A lone fisherman paddled by in a flatbottom boat. Billy pointed to a heron, standing stock-still in the marsh, pretending it was a bent stick. As the fisherman's boat drew near, the bird silently spread its giant wings and flew away.

Sara felt her arms tingle again. She was itching to fly away too. The sky was clear and peaceful. Her stomach rumbled.

"I need chips."

"Race you!" Billy shouted over his shoulder as he sped down the long section of sidewalk that led to the closed-up booths and shuttered shops by the Island airport.

"I beat." He turned his bike by the high wire fence blocking the path. Retracing their way, they headed back towards Centre Island and the main drag. Pumping like crazy to keep up with Billy, Sara could feel her heart pound and flutter. Was that how Maggie had felt when her heart attack happened, only worse, only tighter? She slowed as they glided past Hiawatha Street. Down the block she could see Maggie and Granny Pitts sitting on the lawn, talking. She waved and pedalled on. Maggie was okay. For now, Maggie was okay.

Sitting on a freshly painted park bench, Billy and Sara munched french fries loaded with salt, vinegar and ketchup. The souvenir vendor was washing his windows while his wife re-arranged birch bark canoes with *Toronto Island* stamped on them, and glass snowstorms with skylines of the city inside. Sara had one of these snowstorms on her dresser at home on Dufferin Street.

"Knock, knock!"

"Who's there?" Sara crumpled the greasy paper cone that had held the chips.

"Banana." Billy pulled his big feet out of the way of some passing tourists.

"That's an old one. I don't know why you keep telling old jokes. It's boring." Sara tossed the garbage in the trash barrel at the corner and set off for her bike, chained at the end of Manitou Street.

She glanced back and saw Billy trudging down the street after her. He might have grown a lot since Christmas, but his feelings were still

44

easily hurt. Maybe he wasn't so big after all. He just looked bigger on the outside.

"Truce," she called and pedalled off towards Ward's Island.

"Truce." Billy thrust his leg over the crossbar of his bike and whizzed by her. "Next year I might get a summer job on the ferries."

When he hit the straight stretch he lifted his hands off the handlebars and dropped them to his sides. Sara, speeding up beside him, tried the same thing. Her front wheel went all wobbly. She grabbed the handlebars, pedalled faster and tried again. The bike tipped precariously, then straightened. Sara dropped her hands, grinned, proud of her new talent, and pulled up beside Billy. The two of them, side by side, wheeled down the lakefront, whistling through their teeth.

"You're too young to work on the ferries. Kevin's nineteen."

Sara's voice was drowned out by a roaring engine. The yellow bulldozer was pushing over a small white and blue cottage. Beside it, a heap of trampled daisies, fireweed, marigold and geraniums drooped in the gutter. A crumpled bird's nest and bright blue eggshell fragments lay on the gravel. A rush of anger flooded Sara's face. She pumped like mad until she caught up with Billy.

Tears filled her eyes. What was she going to do? What were any of them going to do?

7

"Are you being a good girl? Don't forget to clean your teeth and change your underwear. Don't stay up too late." Her mother's voice crackled in Sara's ear.

"I do the laundry in that old washer." Sara shifted the receiver to her other hand.

"Watch out for those ringers. One of your aunts caught her thumb. Don't let Maggie do it. How is she?"

"Fine, Mom, we're fine."

"I don't want you and Billy Best running wild all over the Island. I'm afraid without me there you'll do something stupid. You don't have much sense yet. Kids don't."

"How's the baby?"

"He's got the sniffles. Your dad phoned from Montreal. He says the course is really hard and he misses us all." There was a pause on the line.

"The house seems too quiet without you."

"Are you coming out this weekend?" Sara scratched her ankle with her left foot. "There's a regatta."

"I'm worried about John Paul's cold and I don't like to leave the house empty. There are thieves."

"You know that nice white and blue cottage? It's gone." Sara sighed.

"It was run-down anyway. The whole Island is run-down and old-fashioned like the washing machine, Sara. You and Maggie just don't see it."

John Paul screamed in the background. "I've got to run. Be a good girl. Don't let Maggie — "

"I won't let her overdo it, Mom."

Sara replaced the receiver slowly. Maggie looked up from the kitchen counter. She had a tea-towel in her hand.

"I'll do that." Sara grabbed the tea-towel. "You sit down!"

Maggie didn't let go of the towel. Instead she glared at Sara and hung on tight. The two of them stood in the middle of the kitchen floor face to face, eye to eye.

It was like their staring game, where they stared at each other until one of them blinked and laughed, but this time it wasn't funny. Sara didn't know what to do. She felt her teeth clench, her jaw set, her arms strain with the tug on the towel.

"Let go, Sara!" Her grandmother's voice was low and firm.

Sara dropped her end of the towel. Her cheeks burned. She ran out of the kitchen, up the stairs and into her room, banging the door. She threw herself on the bed, scrunching the pillow into a ball, shoving her face into it. What had she done? What had she done that for? What was the matter with her?

She lay there crying. Finally, she wiped her face with the sheet, tidied the bed. She needed to get away, find some place to be alone. She felt rotten. She was a horrible kid.

Sara tiptoed down the fire escape. When she turned the corner of the house, she came upon Maggie, sitting smack-dab in the middle of the walk, coils of rags at her feet, her sewing basket on her lap. "I need more bits cut."

Sara looked down at the sidewalk, blinking furiously. She didn't want to look in Maggie's eyes.

"I'll bring the suitcase out," she whispered.

It was heavy and awkward. She set it up on the picnic table, took the scissors from the back pocket and started cutting strips without saying a word. She had a piece of purple velvet in her hand.

"That's from your grandpa's smoking jacket. He was wearing it when he died."

Sara gulped and raised her eyes, gazing at

Maggie. Her grandma was braiding a long rope of strips together, just as Sara's mother had braided Sara's hair when she was seven or eight.

"He died when your mom was sixteen. Left us on our own, Joe did, without a pension — back then there were no pensions. Your mother had to grow up real fast, poor lassie. Here's a scrap of the dress I made her for the funeral." Maggie held up a long strip of black shiny material. "She wore it to get her first job, too, working for a big trust company down on Bay Street, filing papers."

Sara lifted a bright orange print from the suitcase and cut long strips quickly.

"That's the dress I was going to wear to California, to visit all my daughters, the ones that left with soldiers from the First World War. Lots of jobs down there then, in California. I never went. Except for your Aunt Bea and Beth, none of them have had enough money to come home for a visit. They left me, the way I left my mom, standing on a dock in Scotland, waving."

Sara knew this stuff. Why was her grandma going over it all again now? Why didn't she just bawl her out for grabbing the tea-towel? She knew when Grandpa had died Mom had had to quit school and go to work. She knew she had three California aunts she'd never seen. They sent presents for her birthday. In their pictures, they looked like her mother. All those girls and

49

then Arthur's dad, the only boy.

"Every family has a suitcase full of memories, Sara," Maggie went on. She bent, stitching steadily, the material held close to her face, her glasses sliding down her nose.

"Do you want me to sew?" Sara asked.

"No, I don't, thanks very much." Maggie's eyes behind the glasses widened and she shook her head. "It's my life, Sara, and I've got to stitch it together myself."

Arthur burst through the door, pulling a sweater over his head, singing in a squawky voice, "Goin' to take a sentimental journey, going to set my heart at ease, going to take a sentimental journey to renew old memories."

"I'm glad you didn't choose a musical career, duckie." Maggie put her sewing down. "Leave the singing to the birds."

"Anyone for croquet after supper? Where's Billy?"

Sara nodded to the curtained upstairs rooms.

"See you later, then. Alice and I are going to the regatta." Then he bent over Maggie. "Last one through the wicket is a skunk. Imagine my very own grandmother making light of my musical ability. And to think I've been living with you, lo, these many years."

He kissed the top of Maggie's head, ran and leapt onto his bicycle, pedalling out of sight, humming loudly. Billy stuck his head out the upstairs window. Sara laughed at the rumpled frown, the hair sticking out like porcupine quills. The head disappeared. The curtains closed.

"Why don't you make a cuppa tea, Sara lass?" Maggie said quietly. "We'll cut more strips another day. With any kind of luck I should be able to finish this before summer's over — before the CNE."

* * *

After a long afternoon at the regatta watching canoe races, the menagerie gathered on the lawn. Arthur brought out the croquet set.

Sara chose her favourite mallet, bright red. Maggie beckoned her over.

"Let's strategize." Her dimples dug deeper and she winked slyly. "You whip around as fast as you can. I'll concentrate on knocking their balls into the bushes."

Granny Pitts sat on the sidelines in one of the new lawn chairs with plastic webbing. "Billy, be a pet and bring grandma her sweater from the end of my bed." Billy groaned.

Captain Joe smoked his pipe and watched from under bushy grey eyebrows.

Maggie and Sara were first out of the wicket. Sara tapped her way through the first two hoops before Billy took his shot. He missed with his second and ended up in the deep grass. Arthur hurried through, whamming Sara's ball into Quantz's bushes.

"You did that on purpose," Sara hollered.

"Off my property!" Quantz rose to his full scrawny height. He'd been watering his beloved tomatoes.

Maggie shook her head in disbelief, then wacked Arthur's croquet ball into the currant bushes.

"His bark is worse than his bite." Arthur ran after his ball.

On the last two turns Sara passed Billy but couldn't catch up with Arthur, who clobbered Maggie's ball and went ahead to win. Maggie came second. Sara finished third and Billy brought up the rear.

Sara gave her ball a terrific wallop in the direction of the croquet stand. Controlling that stroke would take practice. She hit it again, back towards the stake. Pow! Back to the croquet stand.

"Careful, Sara, you might hit something." Granny Pitts sucked air in between her teeth. "I'd play too but my heart flutters. I've been taking new pills. The doctor fears regina."

"It's angina, Mrs. Pitts." Maggie pronounced it slowly: *an - ji - na*.

Arthur and Billy started another game of croquet.

"I think you are so brave, Mrs. Shaw," Granny Pitts said to Maggie. "And after a heart attack, too." She pulled a sweater around her skinny shoulders. "Since Mr. Pitts died I've had to watch my health."

Maggie chuckled. "As long as I can keep moving, I will. Sitting still bores me to tears."

"Want me to rub your legs?" Sara hauled the lawn chair close to Maggie's chaise longue.

She started on the left leg and kneaded the calf as if it was a Scottish bap. The rough stockings scraped her hands. Maggie crooned with pleasure as Sara moved to her right leg and worked on the calf and the heel. She didn't know whether it really helped Maggie's circulation, but it seemed to make Maggie happy. That was the main thing.

Granny Pitts went back to crocheting a bedjacket for cold winter nights. Captain Joe snored, his polished sailor boots thrust into the centre of the ring of chairs on the front lawn. The light began to fade in the western sky.

"I whipped Arthur." Billy tossed his mallet into the stand with a clang. "How about scaring lovers in the park, Sara?"

"I'm tired of that old game." Sara remembered the shocked looks on the last pair they had frightened down at Hanlan's Point. The girl's face had gone all blotchy. "I'd rather win at croquet."

So they played another round. Sara kept her eye on the ball this time. She concentrated on moving through the hoops. She held the mallet firmly in both hands. She focussed her whole attention on the game.

"You going to wallop me?" Billy asked as she landed right beside him. Instead she chuckled, tapped his ball sideways and took the extra free stroke to glide to victory. A feeling of satisfaction filled Sara.

"Why not join the big time, kids?" Arthur said as Billy put the croquet set away on the porch. "I'm going bird-watching tomorrow and I need some spotters who can use binoculars. I want to count the ringtailed pheasant population. Interested?"

"How much does it pay?" Billy punched Arthur's arm and pulled up a chair. "Have you read *Pay As You Go* by Ida Nickel?"

"Oooh! That's so bad," Arthur groaned.

"I guess the migration is on." Maggie looked up from her crossword puzzle. "All the Island birds, critters, people are here. Gladys comes tomorrow. We'll all be in our nests."

"We're not birds, Maggie," Sara said sharply, remembering the broken nest on the lakefront by the bulldozer.

"Birds of a feather flock together." Granny Pitts blotted her lips with a lace hankie.

"Birds? What birds?" Captain Joe snuffled, shifting his feet, staring for a moment at the sky. Then he went back to sleep.

"You really started something, Arthur." Maggie headed through the screen door. "Who wants a cuppa tea?"

"Very kind, I'm sure." Granny Pitts cleared her throat.

"Me, too." said Arthur. "Some day there will be a real aviary on the Island — a bird sanctuary."

"What about the people, Arthur? Can we save them?" Sara went in the house to help Maggie with the tea, letting the screen door bang behind her. "Tell Arthur I'll bird-watch tomorrow," she told Maggie, handing her the tray. "I'm going to bed."

"Are you all right?" Maggie asked, touching her shoulder.

"Fine."

Outside, Arthur poured.

"I'll come bird-watching tomorrow if Sara's going," Billy said.

Sara stared through the curtains at her grandma and friends having tea on the lawn. Maggie handed Captain Joe some mussels and crackers. She had fruitcake for Granny Pitts, chocolate Peek Freans for Arthur and Billy. She walked around the whole ring of them. The laughter rose on the air like music.

Down the street, Quantz came struggling with a wheelbarrow full of wood and bricks — from the blue and white cottage on the lakefront.

Sara traced a circle on the pane of glass

closest to her, then put a stick figure of Maggie in the middle. "How do I make sense of it all?"

The sound of talking washed over her. She could feel herself drifting off — and the waves of words coming from the yard felt warm and safe.

8

Sara leaned her back against a young maple tree with light green leaves. The sky shone china-blue over her head, a few trilliums waved in the meadow, their white petals shiny with leftover dew. They are irreplaceable, her science teacher had said. Irreplaceable. Like grandmas, and steamboats, and Island homes.

A duck quacked. Sara lifted the binoculars to her eyes and focussed the lens. These were ter-rific — she could nearly count the feathers, the duck looked so close. Gripping her pencil tightly, she wrote in her notebook. *Ducks — brown, mot-tled, fair sized, maybe mallards*.

A woodpecker hammered high in a beech tree.

Tap, tap, tap. Pause. *Tap, tap, tap*. Sara stood up and followed the sound with the glasses. There he was. She lifted the binoculars for a better look, sharpened the focus. She was getting pretty good at this. Red head, peak of feathers, clinging to the trunk, drilling for his dinner. He cocked his head to one side, silent, as if he knew someone was watching.

Tap, tap, tap. He hammered out his message. Sara wrote the description down and pushed away a growing uneasiness. No matter how hard she tried, big worries niggled like toothaches.

There was a crashing in the woods. "Arthur says it's time to quit and go for ice cream." Billy's face was sunburnt. His freckles had multiplied.

"I need a lemon soda with two scoops of vanilla ice cream," said Sara.

"Did you spot many birds?" Billy reached for her hand to help Sara up. He held it tight. Then blushed and let it drop.

"Ducks, a woodpecker, and a bunch of finches. I didn't spot any ringtail whatnots."

"Pheasants," Billy said.

They walked back through the swampy woods. "I wouldn't want to be a naturalist." Sara chewed a piece of grass. "You have to spend too much time alone. I like people around, like Maggie does."

Billy picked a wild flower with a white moth on it. "Doctors see lots of people." Startled, the moth flew away. "So I won't be alone, either."

Sara knew Billy wanted to be a doctor. He'd

talked about it for as long as she could remember. She scuffed her shoes as they reached the path. Billy tossed the drooping flower away.

"Knock, knock."

"Who's there?" Sara responded.

"Bird."

"Bird who?"

"Bird brain."

"Oh yuck, Billy. Sometimes . . . "

They met Arthur on the sidewalk by the lakefront, where it was very busy. Picnickers carried baskets. A few hardy swimmers passed, carting face masks and flippers.

"Some guy is going to swim Lake Ontario like Marilyn Bell did." Billy unlocked his bike and leapt onto it.

"I'd like to do something spectacular like that." Sara pedalled down the lakeshore, not stopping until she reached the main drag, where comfortable music blared amid hundreds of strolling tourists, and the smell of chips was strong.

Arthur and Billy came sauntering down the middle of the wide boulevard, binoculars hanging, knapsacks on their backs and wrinkled grass-stained clothing on their bodies. Sara smiled.

"You two look like refugees from a safari. I bought the grub."

Arthur pounded his chest like a skinny Tarzan. "Good, Jane, good." The three of them hunched over the white table comparing notes. "Pretty good for beginners."

"The woods are kinda spooky, though," Billy mumbled. "Like reading *Ghost Stories* by I.M. Spooked."

Arthur ignored him and poured more vinegar on his chips. "Once you feel at home in the woods, there's no place like them."

Sara tossed her empty wrapper into the trash. "I'm going home to check on Maggie."

"Don't forget, we're going wading later," Billy shouted after her. "And that's no joke."

"Have to wait an hour. We've just eaten."

"Picky. Picky."

"Am not." Sara struggled with her padlock. She pedalled off.

No birds sang on Hiawatha Street. All the summer people were on the beach, on the main drag, or canoeing on the lagoon. Sara's bike tires made rhythmic clunks as they crossed each crack in the wide grey sidewalk. Out of the corner of her eye she could see old Quantz staking his tomatoes. The sky felt heavy.

Outside Maggie's Sara stopped and listened again. She edged her bike into the stand and locked it, listening for sounds from the kitchen. The same feeling of being alone that she had felt in the swamp filled her. She shivered and walked slowly to the screen door, willing the washing machine to thrash or a teaspoon to clatter. Nothing stirred. Only the ancient refrigerator snapped to attention, filling the darkened hallway with its metal hum.

A plate of fresh oatcakes sat on the table in the spotless kitchen. Where was Maggie?

"Grandma?" Sara called. Her voice sounded thin. She tiptoed into the living room. Nothing was out of place. The clock on the wall ticked slowly, the Chinese lady of the lamp stood silent with her flowers and her parasol. The bags of bits, the beginning rounds of the rug, sat by the couch. Sara's eardrums hurt from listening to the silence.

Maggie Shaw had never been silent or still until recently. She hummed, whistled, rode bicycles, moved furniture, played games. The silence frightened Sara. How long had it been since she had seen Maggie on her bicycle?

Sara felt like two people. The girl with tousled black hair in red shorts and scuffed tennis shoes walked through the quiet house. The real Sara — or was it the shadow Sara? — was outside herself watching, afraid of what that other girl would find behind one of the doors.

"Grandma?" she whispered again, feeling as though a woolly sock were stuck in her throat. She walked back towards Maggie's bedroom. "Grandma?" A whistle-snore broke halfway, turning into a snort. Sara gasped in relief.

"Is that you, Sara?"

Clutching the binoculars around her neck, she followed Maggie's voice as if it was the melody of a rare bird.

"I was napping."

The house emptied of visions. Sara's voice returned. Her shadow disappeared.

Maggie sat propped up on pillows in her bedroom.

"Are you all right?" Sara asked, breathless. She was shaking. "I'll put the kettle on for tea. Right after I go to the bathroom."

"What's all this, lassie?" Maggie crinkled her eyes and smiled.

"We went bird-watching with Arthur, and Billy says I'm getting picky. I don't think I'm picky, do you?"

Sara was sitting on the toilet staring at the typed sign posted on the bathroom door. *FLUSH ONLY WHEN NECESSARY. DON'T CLOG THE TOILET.* Scared. She had been so scared . . .

Sara marched into the kitchen to make the tea. Maggie had beaten her to it.

"Sara, lamb, it's time you and I had a little talk."

Sara's stomach churned like the water by the docks when the ferry pulled out.

Maggie pushed Sara's tea and the plate of oatcakes toward her. Sara grabbed an oatcake and dunked a corner into the steaming cup of tea.

"I'll try not to die when you or I are alone together, but I can't guarantee anything," Maggie said. "I don't want to leave, any more than you want to find me dead. I want to live each day to its full. But I can't do that with you staring at me all the time afraid I'll stop breathing the next minute."

Sara stared at her plate. Her face felt hot. She talked to the clock. "Most of the time, I forget."

Sara turned her eyes back to her grandma's face slowly and discovered she wasn't going to cry after all. Maggie went on. "Why don't we change the job description? Instead of you and I keeping an eye on each other — that's for wee bairns — let's keep each other company. I need the company. I've always needed company."

Maggie came over, stood behind Sara's chair and placed her gnarled hands on Sara's shoulders. "There's a lot of life in the old girl yet."

"That's what Captain Joe says about the *Trillium*." Sara stood to add more hot water to the teapot. She gave her grandmother a quick hug before she grabbed another oatcake.

"No wonder Shaw women are getting taller every generation — comes from eating oatcakes," Maggie giggled. "Pour me another cup of tea.

This one's stone cold. You could read my fortune, you need the practice. No sailboats, though."

Sara beamed. "Maybe there's a tall dark stranger."

9

After supper the next night, the menagerie gathered in the living room. Sara read the bird book her mom and dad had given her. Streaks of lightning crossed the sky. Rain pelted down. Foghorns moaned in the distance.

Gladys Waterby, who'd arrived a few days earlier, came home from waitressing on the main drag and sprawled in the maple rocker. Arthur was reading, the rickety floor lamp casting yellow light over his shoulder. Mr. Best and Billy played gin rummy. Granny Pitts, her skinny legs wrapped in elastic stockings, tiny feet encased in sturdy old-lady shoes, sat resting on the worn armchair with the red Moroccan leather ottoman. Maggie squinted at her stitches. The round rug was growing, overflowing her lap.

"Horrible accident over the Grand Canyon," Gladys sang out gleefully. "Two airplanes collided. All that sky, makes you wonder. They'll have a tough time identifying the corpses. All those bodies strewn over the canyon floor. Won't catch me flying, that's for sure."

"I'd love to fly." Maggie's eyes sparkled behind her bifocals. "Arthur's father was a great flyer."

"Didn't he die in a crash?" Gladys waggled her head.

"He was shot down, Mrs. Waterby. He was a good pilot but there was a war on. I'm just stitching one of his ties into my rug."

Sara glanced at Arthur. He was pretending to read his book but his ears were pink.

"You would have made a great apiary, Mrs. Shaw." Granny Pitts fumbled with her knitting. "Like Amelia Earhart."

"It's aviator, grandma," Billy laughed. "Apiaries are for bees."

"Gin," his dad said and slapped his cards down.

Billy grinned at Sara. "You don't have to be crazy to live here but it helps. *Fun in the Nut House* by Tiny Philbert."

"You're not crazy — you just tell too many dumb jokes."

"Life is serious business," Gladys scolded. "Remember Hurricane Hazel? We had to canoe to the main drag to get groceries."

"Flying would've been be easier," Sara giggled, thinking about her soaring gull. "Maybe I'll be a bird when I grow up."

"They haven't as many brains as you do," Billy hooted. "Even if you do get spooked sitting in the marsh all morning."

"What were you doing in the marsh?" Gladys asked.

"Arthur was teaching us how to bird-watch." Sara tucked in her shirt. "At least the birds get to stay on the Island, no matter what."

"Two men from Metro came to the door yesterday. They heard I might be ready to hand in my lease." Maggie dropped the newspaper on her lap. "I'm not ready yet."

Sara shivered. "They can't make us, can they?"

"All the leases are good until nineteen sixty-eight."

"That's ages. So how come the bulldozer's at work?" Billy asked. "Gin, Dad. I won this time." He came and stood beside Sara.

"Ward's isn't being bulldozed," Billy said.

"They've got more spunk," Arthur said proudly. "They meet and organize."

"Don't be ridiculous. Little people can't change history. If Metro wants this for parkland, there is nothing we can do." Gladys marched out of the room.

The silence was thicker than cream.

Maggie put her finger to her lips. "She'd

rather have life happening in the newspaper. Some of us know it's happening right here." She fished writing paper out of the top drawer of the rolltop desk. "I'll write a letter to the *Telegram*. The rest of you scoot."

"What's the fuss about?" Granny Pitts frowned. "We've been coming to Maggie Shaw's for years. If that Metro chairman, nice man that he is, would just come and see us, he'd understand. Leastways, we don't have to move, do we?"

"Grandma, the bulldozers are knocking down houses," Billy said.

"They haven't come here, have they? We're safe, aren't we?"

"Who knows for how long?" Mr. Best stowed the deck of cards on the bookshelf and left the room.

"Well, summer on the Island is just grand. I always finish off with a trip to the CNE." Granny Pitts picked up her knitting. "Bing Crosby's coming!"

"I love the roller coaster," Billy said. The Canadian National Exhibition, held at the end of every summer in Toronto, was one of his favourite places.

"I love the food building," Maggie chimed in. "I'm like one of Arthur's birds. The CNE is a stopping place on my journey from the Island to the city, from summer to winter."

Sara brought in a tray of teacups, the big

teapot with its knitted cosy, and a plate of oat-meal cookies. Maggie patted the table in front of her and Sara put down the tray. "The doctor said I shouldn't go this year," Maggie sighed. She started pouring tea. Arthur handed round the cups.

"You could if you got better," Sara said loudly. "You're allowed some fun, aren't you?" Then she bit her lip so hard it bled.

Sara hurried from the room, along the dark hallway past the croaking refrigerator, through the screen door and down the street to the beach.

"Me and my big mouth." She kicked sand in the air, bent and picked up some flat stones, skipping them out towards the dark breakwater. Could she build a breakwater around her grandmother?

"Sara, Sara." Billy's voice echoed down the deserted pavement. "I brought your raincoat." He tossed her a yellow slicker.

Sara wiped the tears and drops of rain from her face and jammed her arms in the sleeves. Arthur, his bicycle lantern bobbing on his handlebars, went wheeling by in the mist.

"Let's go buy some chips." Billy hauled a giant flashlight from his pocket. The rain turned to silver threads in its beam.

"I've left Maggie . . . " Sara paused.

"She's okay. She's taking care of Granny Pitts and Captain Joe."

Sara trudged down the sidewalk.

"When I was a kid, I thought all adults were alike," Billy said.

"Well, none of ours are. Gladys doesn't even know what's going on about the Island. Arthur and Alice want to fight."

Billy waved his light around, making big scoops of light in the dark sky. "I'm delivering flyers for them, door to door. You can help."

Sara picked up a stray hunk of granite off the pavement and heaved it toward the lake. It splashed. "I have to find something I can do, something special."

"Like what?"

Sara shook the raindrops from her head, shoved her fists deep into her pockets and slouched down the lakeshore to the main drag.

"Find a way for Maggie to go to the CNE." She felt pulled two ways, toward the lights and music of Manitou Street and by the strange group of people huddled in the living room on Hiawatha. The turmoil inside matched the storm lashing the breakwater. "There's got to be a way."

"It's easier thinking on a full stomach. Come on." Billy took her by the elbow and they both sprinted for the french fries booth.

10

"Come into the city for the day, Sara Jane." Her mother's voice on the phone sounded stern. "Take the nine o'clock ferry." John Paul cried in the background. "I'll meet you at the docks."

"What's your mother want?" Maggie glanced up from stirring the porridge.

"I don't know." Sara filled their orange juice glasses.

"She probably misses you."

"She probably needs help with John Paul or something. Will you be okay?"

"I've got the whole menagerie to keep me company, for the time being."

Sara scooped up a spoon her grandmother had dropped. Maggie Shaw was wearing her old slippers with holes in the toes and the heels run down. She giggled. "I'll buy you a new pair of slippers — if you lend me the cash."

"Might be a waste of money." Maggie sighed, rubbing her left arm. "I sound like glum Gladys. I rented her a room, hoping I could cheer her up, but I've never managed it."

Sara put two Blue Willow bowls, big spoons, the milk jug and the jar of brown sugar on the table.

"Nothing fancy now. We Celts are canny with our pennies." Maggie placed three dollars beside Sara's plate and ladled the oatmeal into their bowls.

"Finish all of it. You want to grow up to be a great-grandmother, don't you?" A spot of milk jiggled on Maggie's chin. Sara leaned across the table and caught it on her serviette.

"Next time you go to town you should buy a new dress, Maggie."

Maggie glanced down at her baggy, faded housedress. "Clothes haven't ever been very important to me, lassie!"

Sara blushed.

"You wouldn't take me to a dog show, right?" Maggie patted Sara's head. "*Thrushima, mo ghaoil*, you'll miss your ferry."

On the dock, Quantz and his girlfriend were talking to two businessmen with briefcases.

"Wait for me!" Sara wheeled past them onto the *Sam McBride* under the bushy wink of Captain Joe.

"Trying out for the Olympic bicycle team, Sara?"

She dashed through the closing accordion gates and up the stairs so she could watch the ferry pull out.

"Looks like Quantz is negotiating with Metro." Captain Joe joined her, leaning his burly arms on the polished wooden railing. "Before long, Centre and Algonquin will be full of ghosts." He heaved a big sigh. "It's bad enough having the *Trillium* sitting idle. What's a sailor to do?"

"Where will you go?" Sara asked.

"Maybe I could find a little spot on Ward's. Metro will never be able to shut it down. The local folks won't let them."

"Like Alice you mean?"

"Her and others. Me, I'd like to save the *Trillium*," the captain went on. "She's the queen of the harbour and deserves better treatment." He tugged on his moustache. "I best go dock this ship. I bet my pay packet that some day the MV *Trillium* will ply these waters again."

The whistle blew, the pulleys cranked, the gangplank slid into place, the ropes were tossed, the sides of the ferry banged against the docks, the water splashed. Behind the whitewashed terminal gate stood Sara's mother, holding John Paul. He waved a pudgy little hand.

Well, what do you know! The kid knew her, he was glad to see her. Inside Sara's chest a funny tickle spread.

Her mother gave her one of her short hugs.

John Paul grabbed her nose. Sara took him from her mother and he wrapped his arms around her neck.

They made their way across the cinder parking lot to the beat-up Mercury.

"Pick up your feet, child. You have the grace of an ape." Her mother unlocked the car door. "Hold the baby."

John Paul smiled and reached for the pen in Sara's shirt pocket. He was turning into a real person. Being a big sister might be okay after all.

Her mother started the car. "We're going to the clinic. John Paul needs his booster shot. Then we'll have lunch."

Walking towards Eaton's, Sara finally spoke. She gulped, "Mom, Maggie wants to go to the CNE. She's always gone since she was a little kid."

"Sara, your grandmother's got to take it easy or she'll die. If you can't figure that out, I'm surprised at you. Maybe you should stay in Toronto and help me with John Paul."

Sara scrunched her shoulders close to her ribs. The pavement before her went foggy.

Her mother pushed the door to Eaton's open. The air filled with the smell of perfumes. Sometimes Sara stopped to try them out. Today the sweetness made her feel sick to her stomach.

"You need a new pair of sandals. Those are scuffed and your big toe hangs over the edge.

What am I going to do this fall?" A frown puckered her mother's forehead.

"I'll get a paper route," Sara said. John Paul clapped his hands together. "I'll be old enough to babysit. I'll buy my own stuff." Sara glanced over at her mother. The frown was fading. "Let's go check the pianos." Sara missed her mom's music.

The smell of polish and wax filled the home furnishing floor. A brand new short-backed piano was on display. A salesman was playing it. Sara's mom walked over.

"It's got good tone. Seems awfully short, though."

"It's the latest home model," the guy said. "Try it."

Her mother's hands flew across the keys. She played a whole bunch of Scottish and Irish songs. Maggie's "You tak' the Highroad" and "Danny Boy" and "Flow Gently, Sweet Afton". Pretty soon a group of people had gathered to listen. Sara's mother's face relaxed, she whispered the words. Her eyes had a faraway look.

John Paul let out a squawk. Ethel Collins came to the end of the song and dropped her hands onto her knees.

"If you ever want a job, come and see me," the salesman said.

"Not bad for someone who never had a lesson." Ethel took Sara's hand in her firm grip and marched down the aisle toward the elevator.

In the Georgian Room the two of them sat at one of the small tables at the side. Sara wiggled her toes up and down in her new sandals. The old ones were in the box, wrapped in tissue. John Paul, in his stroller, chewed on a giant teething biscuit, smiling at them.

"How's Maggie?"

"She's making a giant rag rug out of all those patches she had in the big suitcase. It's already bigger than the one in her front hall. It's going to be immense." Sara ran the ketchup in rings around her macaroni and cheese casserole.

Her mother was playing with the scallops on her plate, lining them up. "She always said she'd make a big one. Waste not, want not. When I was your age we never threw anything out. I hated all that clutter, all that porridge and homemade soup — swore it would never happen to me, never happen to you. The Island house . . . the Island house reminds me. I should come out there, I should . . . "

"We're okay, Mom. You don't have to come." Sara wiped her lips with the napkin.

"Maybe when your dad gets home." Her mother suddenly drew her shoulders together, shovelled the last of her lunch into her mouth.

"He's sent me three postcards." Sara smiled. "Having a busy time, studying hard. Wish I was there."

"The whole family's got to work this summer." Sara's mother sighed. "Maybe next year we can go visit my sisters in California. You can meet your California cousins."

"We could take Maggie," Sara said.

Her mother bent to pick up John Paul's cookie. Her hand fumbled, finally grasped the cookie firmly and gave it back to the baby.

"I wouldn't count on it, Sara."

It was mid-afternoon by the time Sara clambered onto the *Thomas Rennie*. Waiting for the ferry to leave, she leaned against the railing and looked over to the dock where the *Trillium* rode, empty and rocking in the wash from a tugboat. The old ferry's steam engines were silent, the paddlewheels still, the once sanded and oiled decks covered with dust. A stray grey cat, tail waving, walked across the deserted ship, leaving tiny paw prints on the unswept gangway of the retired queen of the harbour.

* * *

Billy came running down the block from the Canoe Club. "I've been helping the guys clean up an old canoe, get it ready to race again. Boy, some of them have muscles. I nearly fell off the dock."

He stood huffing and puffing. Sara sat sprawled in a lawn chair on Maggie's front porch.

"Ever since you got back from the city this afternoon you've been really glum," Billy said.

"I'm busy thinking, okay?" Sara swatted a mosquito.

"Sorry I asked." Billy stomped over to the old swing and pumped like mad until his shoes scraped the clouds.

Arthur whistled as he unlocked his bike. "If anyone wants to know, I'm over at Alice's. She's having a meeting." He pedaled off.

"What about?" Sara hollered after him.

"I heard them talking this afternoon," Billy said. "Alice's neighbours are protesting the lease-buying by Metro. They want extensions. It's all hush-hush."

"Oh." Sara kicked a hole in the grass with her toe.

"Let's go listen," Billy suggested.

"I don't know . . . "

"I'm going. Don't you want to help?"

Sara walked over and hammered the croquet stake. She struck it a heavy blow.

"My goodness, child, you'll split the wood." Granny Pitts shuffled over to her favourite chair. "I'd like to play but my various veins are sore. Billy, be a dear and fetch —"

"Your knitting, right?" Billy leapt off the swing and ran for the stairs. "You aren't the only one who cares about how things work out, Sara Jane Collins," he said as the screen door closed.

Sara shook herself like a dog coming out of the lake.

"I don't know where you young people get all your enmity."

"It's energy, Mrs. Pitts." Maggie settled on the chaise longue. "Enmity is when there is trouble between two people or two factions. That reminds me, Sara, what did your mother have to say?"

"Same old stuff." Sara plopped down again and began flipping the pages of her bird book nervously. Two Chinese lanterns swung in the breeze, casting pink and yellow lights. A few mosquitoes buzzed around, searching for victims.

Maggie pointed down the street to the lakefront. "Look who's coming."

Old Quantz went past, pushing a wheelbarrow full of bricks and wood from one of the demolition sites.

"He's a regular vulture. I never did like that man. He's mean-spirited." Maggie stroked her chin as Quantz wheeled his treasures to his back shed, unlocked the door and disappeared inside.

"There's two kinds of people in my book." Maggie poured herself a cup of tea. "Spenders and hoarders. Quantz works hard at storing up his life, his goods, his property. He has no time for others."

Billy handed Granny Pitts her knitting. She had finished the bedjacket and was making a teddy bear sweater for John Paul.

"You're a spender, Mrs. Shaw." He grabbed an oatcake from the plate.

"What am I, Maggie?" Sara asked.

"What do you think?" Maggie's eyes twinkled in the light from the Chinese lanterns.

"A doctor is a big spender, isn't he?" Billy walked thoughtfully to his bike. "Sara, are you coming to the — " He'd nearly said *meeting* out loud.

Sara shook her head furiously. "Main drag." She finished his sentence.

"Why don't you two hurry off now and have fun?" Maggie winked at them. Then she followed them to the bike rack, leaving Granny Pitts casting off stitches.

Maggie whispered. "If you are going to the meeting, find out if there is anything a fragile old woman can do."

"So much for secrecy." Billy shrugged his shoulders.

"A little conspiracy makes life exciting." Maggie grinned. She gave both their bikes a little tap as they drove off. "Now git, my darlings."

* * *

The streets on Ward's Island lay silent and dark.

"The bulldozers haven't been here." Sara turned down Alice's street. Bikes lined the picket fence. Out in the backyard, sitting on blankets and deck chairs, was a rather motley group of people. Billy and Sara slid into the back row.

"My parents settled here in eighteen eighty-six. I'm not moving," one old fellow shouted.

Alice, sitting on the ground beside the editor of the Island newspaper, spoke. "Saying we won't go isn't enough."

"We could write and phone our alderman."

"We should convince people from the other boroughs of Metro that the whole idea is ridiculous."

"What about a petition?"

"I thought when the city handed us over to Metro that we'd get a fairer deal."

"Maybe we should sell while we have the chance and clear out."

"No." A chorus of voices filled the air.

"I'll head the building committee. If we fix up our places, they can't say nasty things about our community being run-down."

"Bring all your stories to me and I'll publish them," the editor said.

"I'll head the publicity and promotion committee," Alice volunteered. Soon everyone in the room had put up their hands to join some committee.

"We need to meet weekly to look at strategy," Alice was saying.

"Maggie's good at strategy," Sara said out loud.

"Aren't you Maggie Shaw's granddaughter? It's great to see the next generation coming along," the old pioneer said.

Sara blushed. Billy walked over to talk to the

guy on the building committee.

"Tea and coffee are served." Arthur appeared at the door with a tray of steaming mugs. Sara passed out the cups.

"Hey, what about a game of *Monopoly* after this gang is gone? Just the four of us." Alice piled two plates dangerously full of chocolate brownies.

* * *

The *Monopoly* game was over. "I had a winning strategy," Sara announced, after she'd won. "Spend when it's to your advantage, and save for the tough corners."

Then she paused, listening to herself. Maybe she could act like that in real life, storing up the good stuff — John Paul knowing her and turning into a real kid, her mom talking to her as if she was a big girl, and Alice and Arthur trying to save the Island — for the tough times which always seemed to come in between.

11

"We haven't walked the breakwater yet." Billy gnawed a peanut butter sandwich and swung in the hammock. "And the summer's nearly over."

The house on Hiawatha Street seemed sleepy. Maggie had gone to the city to meet her daughter and to see her doctor. Everyone else had left for work except for Granny Pitts who liked sleeping in.

Billy loosened his sandals and rolled up his pant legs. "Ready? *Beat the Heat* by Wade A. Lake."

"Sure." Sara shook her head in disbelief. "Try *Puddle on the Floor* by I. P. Standing."

"No fair, that's an old one."

"Well, I don't see why you have to make corny jokes."

"I get nervous."

"What about?" said Sara.

"I don't know. It's just there seems to be too much going on and I can't help feeling something bad is going to happen."

"So you tell jokes?"

"Yeah, so I tell jokes." Billy sighed.

The morning water was calm. They waded out to where the spit of sand nearly reached the giant boulders. The water was cool but not impossible. Out in the lake a fishing boat tooted. They waved. Two huge tankers slid silently by on the horizon. The grey-green water met the blue sky at what seemed a very long distance away.

Sara jumped to the next rock. She slipped off, dipping her pantleg in the shallow water sloshing down below.

Waves from the tanker splashed over Sara's bare feet. A gull screamed as the two kids scampered down the rocks.

"That gull doesn't like us much." Billy reached across and helped Sara onto a particularly high rock.

"Beebee — " Sara began as the two of them sat down on a flat rock to rest. Billy tossed pebbles into the water. They made a thuddy sound like a deep note from a tuba.

"You haven't called me that for ages," said Billy.

"Sometimes I feel like a little kid, you know."

"Me too."

"You're big now," Sara said.

"Yeah. But I keep bumping into things."

"Oh. I thought I was the only one."

"Maybe it's both of us." Billy grinned.

Sara sighed and scrubbed some green algae off the rock. A wave washed it away. "Dad says the Island will never be the same," she said.

"That's the trouble. See. I was just coming out to have my normal great summer. It's not fair."

"Maybe life isn't." Sara pushed the bangs out of her eyes and stood up, stretched out her arms like a tightrope walker and picked her way down the rocks. She slid off once, making a big splash. She scrambled up and walked gingerly to the end of the breakwater.

When they got home, Maggie was back from the doctor's. She was wearing her loose-fitting housedress again. Her stockings wrinkled on her calves. Sara shook her head. If she did find a way of taking Maggie to the CNE, she'd have to do something about the way she dressed. Funny, you could love somebody buckets but they could still embarrass you. Her mother shouted at kids and dogs who crossed the yard, her dad wore stupid brown shoes that nobody else wore, Arthur made smart remarks around her friends, and Billy told dumb jokes. And what did she do — maybe disappear into to her room, run away to the beach? Maybe her friends noticed those things, and minded.

As Sara came down the stairs, dressed to go out with Billy to get bait for their fishing trip the next day, Gladys was reading. "A Polish tanker sank on the East coast. Collided with another ship. Over fifty lives lost. Imagine all those people, their bloated bodies floating in the water."

"Death by accident is better than death by design," Captain Joe said. "Reminds me of the story of Radanmuller, the lighthousekeeper here over a hundred years ago." The *s* in *years* whistled. His voice took on a mysterious tone.

"I'd forgotten about the murder," Maggie laughed. "You haven't told the story for at least a year, Joe. Stop munching those herring and crackers and tell Gladys. She loves crime. Don't forget the ghost, too."

"Let's get out of here, Billy," Sara whispered. "All I need right now is Gruesome Gladys calling up the ghost of Radanmuller. He'd show up in my dreams with his head all bashed in, like his drinking or smuggling buddies left him." Sara giggled. She and Billy had heard the story of Radanmuller many times before.

"Especially on a dark and stormy night when we're going wandering along eerie canals." Billy shivered.

"Did you say the Erie Canal or the eerie canal?"

"Take your pick!"

Night sounds welcomed them — owls, crickets, frogs, slow-moving outboards. The Harbour Police launch rocked on the far bank of the lagoon, its engine running.

"What are you guys watching for?" Billy hollered.

"Looters," one of the officers called.

"We're getting worms," Sara shouted.

"They should check out Quantz's woodshed." Billy scooped up nightcrawlers with a teaspoon. The earth was dark, rich and soft. Miniature volcanoes showed exactly where the worms were.

"Worms have some job, eh?" Sara nudged Billy. "Regurgitating earth so it becomes fertile soil. Like doing dishes — it's a dirty job but someone has to do it."

The water lapped against the cribbing. The two of them made their way along the lagoon to where a neighbour's cruiser was tied. Sara could hear the faint putt-putt of an outboard motor headed away from them towards the Gibraltar lighthouse.

"Must be the ghost of Radanmuller," Billy joked.

"Stupid. He was killed in the winter, so he'd be on a sled. It's probably someone going night fishing."

"Let's go after them," Billy whispered. "If I go home, Granny will need me to fetch something."

"Who do you think we are? Nancy Drew and company?"

"The Hardy Boys," Billy giggled. "But we don't go jetting all over the world to solve mysteries."

"Just rowing along a dark lagoon with a ghost." Sara helped Billy put their dinghy into the water. They got in and paddled out from the shore. Sara slipped the oars into the oarlocks and started to row. She loved the way the little boat moved as she pulled. With each stroke of the oars she felt power surge through her arms and her legs. To swing higher, to cycle farther, hit the croquet ball straighter, row faster — all seemed awfully important this summer. Sara set her jaw and pulled rhythmically. Reach. Stroke. Pause. Reach. Stroke. Pause.

Lights bobbed about fifty metres ahead. Voices mumbled. The smell of seeping gasoline hung sweet and heavy on the air. The moon came out from behind a cloud.

"Looks like Quantz's motorboat," Billy said. "Give me the oars. I'm faster." The two of them switched places, rocking the little boat as they crawled about. Sara perched on the prow.

"Looks like Quantz and his girlfriend. Maybe we'd better go back."

"Don't be a wet noodle." Billy pulled on the oars with all his might.

"I don't like the feel of it."

"Trust me," Billy said. "And pass a life-jacket."

Billy rowed until the motorboat was back in sight. An owl hooted in the elms. Tree shadows along the banks of the lagoon shimmered in the moonlight.

They rounded a bend in the channel and glimpsed the lighthouse shedding its green light. Quantz was tying his boat to the dock close to the whitewashed lighthouse keeper's cottage. A water taxi rocked in the swell on the other side of the dock.

"They're meeting someone," Sara whispered. "It's like a hundred and fifty years ago."

"You sound like Gladys with the nightmare news." Billy punched Sara's shoulder.

"What if they see us?"

"They'll never even know we're around." Billy beached the dory, tying it to an iron ring on the rocky shore. Sara and he picked their way over sharp stones to the back of the cottage. They scrambled up onto a rock leaning near the clothesline. A crooked shutter in the kitchen window gave them a good view of the inside.

Quantz and his girlfriend sat at a bare wooden table with two greasy guys. They were drinking rye whisky. The bottle stood in the centre of the table. A stained gunny sack leaned beside Quantz's left foot.

Quantz reached down and pulled a filthy

yellow towel out of the sack and unrolled it. A small crystal chandelier and two brass light fixtures tumbled out.

"That's from the hotel," Sara gasped.

The two strangers shrugged their shoulders. One pulled a couple of bills out of his wallet.

Quantz, face red, leapt to his feet.

"He's not happy," Billy said.

"He never is," Sara whispered, realizing she was excited.

A chair fell over. Everyone stood. Quantz slugged back the rest of his whisky and walked right up to the guy with the wallet. He shoved his fist in the guy's face.

Sara croaked, "Do you think that's the same keg of booze in the corner, the one Captain Joe says Radanmuller had?"

"It would have rotted by now, silly," Billy chided.

"Like Radanmuller's body." The rock they were balancing on teetered. Sara reached out a hand to steady herself and pushed against the window. The glass shattered. She screamed. Billy fell and crumpled in a heap on the ground.

Sara jumped down and helped Billy up. The two of them lit out for the dinghy.

The back door of the cottage hurled open and Quantz and his friend ran screaming and waving down to the beach. Without a word, the two kids untied the boat and shoved off.

"You'll have to row, Sara," Billy moaned. "I've hurt my foot." Sara picked up the oars. Her ears filled with thunder. Her chest was doing somersaults. Her hand ached and blood dripped from it.

The police launch roared past and nosed into the dock just as Quantz, his friend and the pair from the city climbed into their boats.

"Stay where you are. We are coming aboard," one of the officers hollered through a bullhorn.

"Wow!" Sara braced her feet against the crosspiece on the bottom of the dinghy and pulled. Every muscle in both arms ached. She rowed down the lagoon like the devil was after her. Billy clutched the sides of the boat and looked sick.

"Can you walk?" Sara secured the dory to their neighbour's cruiser, and left the full can of wiggling worms on their deck. She supported Billy and they struggled back to Hiawatha Street.

"Where have you two been?" Billy's dad shouted from the front porch. In the house all the lights were blazing. To Sara it looked like the best place in the whole wide world.

"You've had us all worried," Mr. Best scolded, then noticed Billy's limp and Sara's hand. "Oh my gosh, what happened?"

Soon Sara's cuts were bandaged and she was holding a steaming cup of hot chocolate in her good hand. Maggie had phoned the doctor. "He'll be right over. I'm sure glad Dr. Wright spends summers out here."

"Oh, what a strategy." Granny Pitts sat wringing her hands.

"That's tragedy." Maggie popped bread into the toaster.

"That's what I said. What if Billy's broken his ankle?"

Sara patted the old woman's arm. Maggie made cinnamon toast. Mr. Best cleaned the blood from Billy's scraped and swollen ankle. Billy groaned.

Granny Pitts leaned towards Billy. "If walking is too hard, we'll commandant a wheelchair."

"Commandeer, Mother Pitts," Mr. Best laughed. "We could rent one."

That's when the great idea popped into Sara's head. Sitting there, wet, sore and worn out, with the menagerie around her, with Maggie stirring sugar into Billy's cocoa, Sara knew how to grant Maggie her wish.

"I know how to get Maggie to the CNE, Billy," she whispered as the doctor knocked at the door.

12

Next morning, Sara woke with a start. She could hear Arthur scraping the porridge pot in the kitchen and she needed to talk to him. She pulled on her red shorts and white jersey, and ran a comb through her hair.

"Arthur, I know how to get Maggie to the CNE, and Billy too, if he's still off his foot."

Arthur looked up from his toast and jam. "I thought your mom and the doctor said no. They're afraid Maggie would get worn out." He wiped his mouth with a serviette and stood. "Look, I've got to leave."

Sara was jumping from one foot to the other with excitement. "But —"

"Why don't you walk me to the ferry and explain your idea? But you'll have to walk fast."

Hiawatha Street filled with sound as the two cousins ran from the house. Robins chattered. A squirrel made warning trills. Nero, Quantz's dog, began barking loudly. Quantz's face appeared at his front window. He shook his fist at Sara as she and Arthur passed.

"He thinks Billy and I ratted on him. We didn't though. The Harbour Police must have had him under surveillance."

"I'd watch out for him if I were you. He'll carry a grudge." Arthur began jogging. "Hurry up, will you? Captain Joe isn't going to hold the ferry for me."

Sara sprinted to keep up with him. Her bones ached from last night's fall and her hand tingled where the cuts were. "Granny Pitts said Billy could use a wheelchair if his leg is broken."

"So?" Arthur cut across the park towards the ferry docks.

"Don't you see? We could rent a chair for Maggie. Then Mom couldn't complain. Neither could the doctor, could he?"

"But how would we get her to the CNE?" Arthur mopped his forehead with his white handkerchief.

"How are you and Alice getting all that stuff for the "Save the Island" booth there?" Sara asked.

"My boss is lending me his van for the day."

"Would he mind if you took us?"

"I don't think so."

"So you won't get in trouble?" Sara grinned.

The horn on the ferry tooted.

"You'll help?" Sara and Arthur sprinted the last few metres. Captain Joe waved them on board.

"We'll work out the details."

"Cutting it pretty close, you two." Captain Joe shook his head. He smelled of herring in wine sauce. "Where are you going, Sara?"

"For the ride. I figured out how to get Maggie to the CNE. Arthur's going to help."

Captain Joe shoved his blue cap to the back of his head and scratched his grey hair. "Can I help, too?

"You could push one of the wheelchairs."

"Are you sure I don't qualify for sitting in one?" He laughed. The ferry sliced its way through the waves in the bay. The diesel motor hummed. Arthur and Sara filled him in on the details.

"It's kind of a closing celebration," Arthur said. "Sara's gift to Maggie."

Sara blushed.

"Too bad we couldn't take the grand old lady of Centre Island to the fair in the grand old ferry of the Great Lakes. The *Trillium* sits idle in her berth. I hate to see the old girl beaten like that." Captain Joe cleared his throat and pulled his pipe out of his pocket, knocking it on the railing. A few shreds of tobacco drifted down.

"Nothing's over until it's over," Arthur said.

He waved as he flew down the stairs to the gangway that was filling with commuters waiting to disembark.

Sara watched Arthur stride toward the red and yellow streetcars. She felt tingly inside with plans.

Captain Joe appeared at her elbow. "Look, I've got a break. Why don't we go take a stroll around the *Trillium* while you're waiting for the next trip? Do you want a soda pop?"

"Milk and a donut." Sara followed him to the coffee vendor's counter.

After they had cleaned up their crumbs, Sara and the captain made their way across the docks to the berth where the *Trillium* rocked, its paint peeling, its brass fittings tarnished, its sign hanging crooked. The stray grey cat meowed as they hauled themselves over the side and jumped down on the dusty deck.

"When I was a little kid, I loved going downstairs to the engine room. Those steel rods going up and down always made me think of huge metal knees." Sara sighed. "They looked so strong — like they'd never stop."

"Let's go take a gander."

Silently, they leaned their elbows on the brass railing and stared at the stilled steam engine. The bottom of the ship was filled with oily water. A faint smell of dirt and old paint hung in the air.

"I miss the old girl," Captain Joe muttered.

Memory played a trick on Sara. Just for a moment she heard the thrum of the engine, the splash of the water, the dance of the wood and steel and paddle wheel as they meshed together to send the ship scurrying across the harbour.

"Can't old ferries be fixed?" Sara's voice came out in a whisper.

Captain Joe shrugged his shoulders. "Launched in nineteen-ten, operated for forty-six years, left to rot in nineteen fifty-six. Sure, the *Trillium* could be restored. But it would take close to half a million dollars."

"Maybe you should write letters to the editor and politicians. Maggie does. She could show you how." Sara took her hankie and rubbed the brass railing in front of her until it shone. "Maybe you should buy a boat of your own. You could park on the lagoon like our neighbours do."

"Harrumph!" Captain Joe made his way up the stairs to the main deck. The wash from the *Thomas Rennie* made the *Trillium* heave and rock. The skinny grey cat rubbed against his pant leg. The captain reached into his bulging pocket and brought out a small jar of pickled herring.

"Here, kitty," he said. "Eat, cat, keep up your strength. You'll need it if you're going to survive. It's a tough world out there." And then to himself, "Buy a boat of my own, now there's an idea. . . .

Buy a boat of my own."

Sara pushed the hair out of her eyes, smoothed it behind her ears and sprang over the side. "Don't say anything to the rest of the menagerie about taking Maggie to the CNE, okay? It's still a secret." She ran for the *Thomas Rennie*, leaving the Captain and the cat keeping each other company.

* * *

"Where have you been so early in the morning?" Maggie asked as Sara flew through the door.

"I've figured out how to get you to the CNE. We can use a wheelchair. Captain Joe and Arthur are going to help. It's a closing celebration." Sara bounced up and down on the balls of her feet.

Maggie paused with her teacup halfway to her mouth, her brow wrinkled. "Oh, I get it," she grinned. Dimples creased her cheeks. "If little kids get to ride in strollers to save their legs — why not grannies in wheelchairs?"

"And stupid teenagers who hurt their ankles," Sara added.

Maggie gave Sara a big hug. "Have I told you lately that I love you?"

"Should we tell Mom?"

Maggie paused.

"She might stop us," Sara went on.

"Your mother's a great woman, don't get me wrong, now. But this is our summer." Maggie put her hand on her granddaughter's shoulder. The warmth of it gave Sara a rosy feeling.

"Arthur and Alice, Captain Joe, Billy, and you and I can all go together. Alice is running the "Save the Island" booth," she said.

"We'll have to strategize!" Maggie whispered happily. "I'm glad Arthur's found such a fine girl. Reminds me of myself when I was younger. If families don't grow their own free spirits, best they go out and marry some."

Maggie was sitting at the table taking deep breaths and fanning herself with her writing pad. Every time Maggie did that it made Sara's knees feel like jelly. She gulped and looked away as her grandmother took one of her little pills. "Let's get to work on the plan, shall we?" her grandmother said.

Sara swept the few crumbs from under the chairs onto the dustpan and threw them into the garbage.

"I could get a doctor's appointment and insist that you take me — with Arthur's help, of course," Maggie went on.

"Arthur's renting a wheelchair and borrowing his boss's van," said Sara.

"Can we stay long enough to eat at Shopsy's?"

"We'll figure it out." Sara patted Maggie's hand.

"This feels quite naughty," Maggie chuckled. The colour had come back into her cheeks. "What about Billy? We don't want Granny Pitts blab-bing. Besides, she might suffer from pulpata-tions in a big crowd like the CNE."

"Palpitations, Maggie. It's palpitations."

"I know, I get them myself." Maggie was staring out the window at the robins feasting in the bushes. "Saying goodbye isn't easy."

Sara laid her hand on top of Maggie's. "It's just a little adventure. The fall will be great, too."

"I don't feel any older now in my head than I did when I emigrated. Something about crossing the harbour reminds me of how many shores I have left."

"We'll be back before bedtime. In time to watch the fireworks," Sara said. *Please don't talk like that, Maggie*, she said in her head. I'll get scared again. She blinked and put the milk away in the rumbly refrigerator.

The doctor's station wagon pulled up in front. All the neighbours came out to watch. Billy got out, leaning on his father's arm, his leg below the knee encased in plaster. He hobbled up the walk, grinning at Sara, who held open the screen door.

"A lot of fun in the water you are going to be," Sara laughed. "Canoeing, anyone?"

"Oh, shut up," Billy said.

Quantz, watching from his garden, dug around his rhubarb plant with a vengeance.

"That guy sure hates us." Billy winced as he hauled himself into the house. *"The Case of the Broken Leg* by Frank Lee Eiffel."

Maggie chuckled and put on the kettle.

"I got ten stitches and two broken bones."

"How are you going to percolate?" Granny Pitts wrung her hands.

"Perambulate, Granny," Billy sighed.

"We'll get a wheelchair and I'll push him," Sara said.

"Nothing new in that," Billy said. "You're always trying to push someone around."

"Am not!"

"Are too."

"Am not."

"Hush, you two," Maggie scolded. "What's the news?" she asked Mr. Best.

"Quantz has been charged with looting, the others with trafficking in stolen property. They have been arraigned until September."

"So he's free."

"Under his own recognizance." Mr. Best, conscious of Billy and Sara's puzzled frowns, went on. "He has to keep himself out of trouble until the hearing. By the way, the bowling alley is closing."

"I thought we were fighting back?" Maggie came in carrying a tray of salmon sandwiches and tea.

"Win some and lose some, I guess." Mr. Best helped himself to a sandwich. Maggie nodded in agreement.

"Somehow I was hoping that filling the house

101

this summer, same as every other year, would mean I could count on things carrying on."

"What about the CNE?" Billy whispered.

Sara raised her finger to her mouth. "Later, dummy." She nodded in the direction of Gladys and Granny Pitts. "They might tell."

13

Sara and Arthur pulled up the croquet hoops and stored them in the shed. Billy looked so forlorn sitting on the sidelines that they'd stopped playing. Maggie dozed over her braided rug. Mr. Best had gone on a buying trip for Eaton's.

Alice rode up on her bike. Arthur, coming around the side of the house, ran to meet her. They hugged.

"Geez, what a pair of lovebirds." Billy giggled. He'd been sitting in his wheelchair reading a novel. "Hey, Sara, how about you and me? Give me a kiss. Will you be my girlfriend?"

"Don't be a drip." Sara punched him on the arm.

"Ouch!"

Alice and Arthur glanced around, making sure no one other than the CNE team were in earshot before they spoke.

"Look, we have to be careful not to give the game away," Arthur said.

"Gladys cornered me in the drug store the other day," Alice explained. "She wondered if we were planning some big demonstration about the Island."

"The other morning at breakfast she complained about all the whispering," Arthur added.

"She asked me if everything was all right," Sara said.

"It's a good thing it's only a few days until we go."

"Too bad the summer's nearly over. I don't want to go home," said Sara.

"None of us do." Billy sounded sad.

"I'll stay on with Maggie," Arthur said. "We'll close up the house, pack everything away. I'll keep an eye on Maggie and stay — "

"Close to me." Alice took his arm.

"I hear wedding bells." It was Maggie, awake from her doze, a big smile creasing her face. Then a shadow followed. "Soon, I hope. Make it soon."

"I'm going for ice cream before I get sick." Sara stalked off toward the lakeshore.

Down at the beach, she searched for flat stones and skipped them over the water. It was getting late and the moon cast shadows on the lake. Sometimes the menagerie was too much, thought Sara. Maybe I should be a hermit. Why do I always walk away from things?

She shook her head and sauntered off towards the main drag. When she got there, under the first street lamp sat Billy Best, cast, wheelchair, and all.

"We're suffering from the end of summer blues. That's Dr. Best's diagnosis. Calls for a double scoop sundae with chocolate syrup." Billy wheeled ahead of Sara, showing off his new arm muscles.

Captain Joe passed them with Kevin the deck-hand, heading towards the yacht club. "Going for mussels, toast and a brew," he said, winking. "And following up a lead. Some young lady I know gave me a great idea."

* * *

Expedition evening was like the night before Christmas. The team gathered close to the wood-shed to go over the plan as soon as Granny Pitts had gone to bed and Gladys had headed off to the main drag for coffee.

"Okay." Arthur pointed at Sara.

"At seven forty-five, I get up and wake Captain Joe, Billy, Arthur and Maggie."

"I'll probably be awake already," Maggie said.

Arthur took over. "At eight fifteen, Alice arrives and the two of us make sandwiches for our lunch."

"I make toast and coffee for everyone," Sara broke in.

"I talk to Ethel on the phone. Tell her I'm leaving for the doctor's." It was Maggie's turn.

"We catch the nine o'clock ferry, the *Sam McBride*. I wish it was the *Trillium*," Captain Joe said.

"We can't have everything," Maggie said. "What an adventure."

Arthur hurried on. "Captain Joe, carrying the lunch and supplies, leads the parade. Sara pushing Billy, Arthur pushing Maggie, and Alice pulling the posters and petitions for the Island display in Billy's old wagon come after."

"Arthur drops Maggie and Sara at the doctor's, Billy at school to register. Captain Joe and Arthur go on to the CNE with me and the display," put in Alice.

"I pick each of you up between eleven and eleven thirty, returning to the Queen Elizabeth gates at noon," said Arthur.

"After lunch on the picnic grounds we separate and see the exhibits."

"Anyone getting tired or wanting to help comes to the Island booth for a break. I'll be there all day." Alice swatted a stray mosquito.

"Okay, everyone. It's time to get off to bed. Tomorrow is a big day." Arthur put his arm around Alice and the two of them walked away wheeling her bike.

Sara couldn't sleep, so she packed her bag for home. Mom and Dad were coming to pick her up on Sunday, two days after their excursion to the CNE. School started Tuesday. She tiptoed around her room picking stuff up, folding it.

"Is that you, Sara?" Maggie called from the hallway. "Turn off your light and go to sleep."

* * *

Friday, September 2, 1956. The weather was perfect, warm not hot, blue skies with white puffs of clouds like pale candy floss, light breezes smelling of marigolds and fresh cut grass. Lake Ontario stretched calm and unruffled as the *Sam McBride* glided across the harbour.

Ethel phoned to check on the doctor's appointment, and told Sara to take Maggie home right after. "Just make sure she doesn't overdo it," she cautioned before hanging up.

The CNE team made quite a sight leaving the Island house, two in wheelchairs and two pushing.

Maggie's eyes sparkled behind her glasses. She had come down the stairs after breakfast wearing a bright black and white print dress that Ethel had bought her on sale in the Annex. It was the right size, for a change. "How do I look? It's the new slim version of Maggie Shaw." She twirled in the centre of the kitchen floor. "I don't want to embarrass my granddaughter."

Sara blushed.

"You look great, Maggie," Arthur grinned. And they set off.

"I'm not spending all day in the food building," Billy said.

"Well, I'm not spending all day looking at cars and boats," Sara retorted, as she pushed his chair over a bump.

"Okay, pipe down. I can't think with you two squabbling. Transporting rare birds would be easier," Arthur quipped.

"You tak' the high road and I'll tak' the low road and I'll be in Scotland afore you. For me and my true love will never meet again on the bonnie bonnie banks of Loch Lomond," Maggie sang as Arthur wheeled her toward the dock. In her new dress, pearls, perky straw hat and tidy nylons and shoes, she could have been the queen mother.

"One of my old Scots friends told me the high road was the faerie road." Maggie patted Sara's hand. "I'm wondering if we're going that way, lassie, you and I?"

Sara and Maggie were the first to be let off. They left the wheelchair in the van and mounted the stairs to the doctor's office.

"Oh, Mrs. Shaw," the receptionist smiled. "It will just be a few minutes. Is this your granddaughter?"

"This is Sara," Maggie beamed.

"I would have known you anywhere. You look like your grandmother. Have you had a good summer?" the nurse asked.

Maggie and Sara nodded together. "We sure have."

"You're all dressed up today, Mrs. Shaw. What's the occasion?"

"We've a big date, Sara and I." Maggie winked. She led the way to two chairs close to the coffee table. Sara picked up an old *Reader's Digest*. Maggie looked over her shoulder. They both liked the "Humour in Uniform" jokes.

"Yeah." Sara couldn't help herself — she had to tell someone of her victory. "We're off to the CNE, Maggie and I."

"Are you sure?" The nurse went tut, tut.

"It's okay. We're using a wheelchair. Maggie will be safe and sound." Sara grinned from ear to ear.

"The doctor will see you now, Mrs. Shaw."

Arthur came back for them promptly at eleven fifteen. Just as the van pulled away, the receptionist waved from the window.

"Did you forget anything?" Sara asked.

"No. Did you?" Maggie frowned.

"Maybe she's just being friendly. Do you want to go back and see what she wants?" Arthur asked.

"No," Maggie whispered.

"What did the doctor say, Maggie?" Arthur studied her face in the mirror as he drove to Billy's school.

"He thinks I should go into hospital again.

109

I'm not ready yet." She sighed.

The van pulled up in front of Bloor Collegiate. Billy sat waiting.

"Wow, you should see my homeroom teacher. She's beautiful."

"Boy, are you getting dippy about girls!" Sara banged the door as he was loaded into the van.

"Your turn will come," Maggie said.

"Your turn will come," Arthur said.

"Is there an echo in here?" Sara asked.

"Methinks the lady protests too much." Arthur chuckled. He and Maggie exchanged glances.

Arthur pulled in front of the Queen Elizabeth gates.

The van moved slowly over to the high columns, the impressive iron gates. "Here we go, just like royalty," Arthur whispered, patting Maggie Shaw's shoulder.

"Not quite," Sara gasped. A policeman with huge white gloves was waving them over. Standing beside him, with fire in her eyes, stood Sara's mother.

"Oh, oh." Sara grabbed Maggie's hand. "What do we do now?"

14

"Where do you think you are going?" Sara's mother shouted. "Who's responsible for this?" John Paul let out a wail, frightened by the noise.

Sara and Maggie stood side by side, heads bowed. Arthur helped Billy out of the van and into his wheelchair. Then he rolled Maggie's chair behind her so she could sit.

"How could you, Sara, after what I told you? Arthur, I thought you would show more sense." Ethel stood before the three culprits shaking her fist. "Making colossal fools out of the whole family. If I hadn't phoned the doctor this morning, I never would have known."

Sara bit her lip. Trust her to blab to the doctor's receptionist. Arthur shifted his feet. Maggie cleared her throat. She sat down slowly in the wheelchair. "It's my fault. I don't like confrontation. I'd rather run away."

Sara, listening — holding herself together with tight muscles, stiff bones — took in Maggie's words. So she wasn't the only one in the family with the run-away problem. She and Maggie had that in common. Only this time it had caught up with them.

"I only want to protect you, Mother," Ethel protested.

Sara and Arthur glanced at each other. Billy rolled over to join them. "Maybe we should have told."

"Never mind, Billy," Maggie said firmly. "This is between Ethel and me. I have to face up to it."

"We could talk this over in private, at home on Dufferin Street." Ethel looked around at the cluster of gawking spectators, the policeman, the menagerie.

Embarrassed, some of the crowd shuffled off toward the CNE entrances. Captain Joe came through the gates to join them.

Arthur stepped forward. "I think we need to finish this here. Maggie's not alone."

Ethel clutched the handles of John Paul's stroller. She looked flustered.

Maggie pulled herself up to her full height. "No, Ethel, we are not going home to discuss this. I'm going to the CNE. Sara has arranged a great day."

"Very well, Mother." Ethel grabbed Sara by

112

the hand. "But Sara's coming with me. She has to learn her lesson."

"What lesson is that, Ethel?" Captain Joe asked. "That helping others realize their dreams isn't good? That overcoming obstacles isn't good? That kid's a real little trouper. You should be proud. With any kind of luck she'll grow up to be just as determined as you are."

He took his pipe out of his pocket and started filling it with tobacco. A faint smile danced across his face.

"If you've got a sweater and some spare diapers you could join us." Maggie put a calming hand on her daughter's shoulder.

Ethel sighed and rocked the stroller back and forth a couple of times. Sara looked up into her mother's face. Her heart was in her mouth. Her feet itched, telling her they wanted to run to the van or to the family car, to get away. Maggie sat back down, hands clutching the arms of the wheelchair. Sara took a big gulp of air.

"You could keep a keen eye on Maggie if you came with us, Mom." The whole group stood silent, waiting.

Ethel studied the team. "I don't have a ticket."

"I'll get you one." Arthur sprinted to the sales window.

"I still think it's foolishness." Ethel turned slowly and walked to the car, rummaging in the back for baby supplies.

"Hurry," Maggie said quietly to the assembled team. "Sara, skeedaddle with Billy."

"Let's try our luck at the shooting gallery," Billy suggested. "I could win you a big panda." He reached his hand up and covered Sara's.

"I was afraid there for a couple of minutes."

"I thought for sure you'd have to go home." Billy pointed ahead. "Look, the food building, wonder of wonders."

"I need a chocolate fix. Let's go to Hershey's or Lowry's and get free samples."

"Swifts is giving away a hundred free hams today. Maybe we could get one. We're a couple of hams," Billy grinned.

Sara wheeled him past the balloon sellers, jugglers, hot dog vendors, candy apple and candy floss makers, up the ramp to the food building.

"I'm not staying too long. I want to look at new cars."

"Okay! Okay!"

"I can get my learner's next year. Take you for a spin, with Dad along of course," said Billy.

Sara took a big swig of free cola. Her bag of posters and free samples was full.

"I'll go to the car show now," she said.

Billy oohed and aahed and talked about the horsepower in the all-new Chevrolet. Sara fell in love with a little mini car from Britain. It cost just over a thousand dollars. "That's my kind of car."

"It's a glorified tin can, but I got all the

specs for you," said Billy.

As they left the car show and headed for a park bench, Billy wheeled himself ahead of Sara.

"Where are you going?"

"The midway," Billy hollered over his shoulder. "I want to go to the Haunted House."

Sara ran, grabbed the handles of his wheelchair and gave him an incredible push.

At the midway, the giant laughing woman wiggled and jiggled on her stand. Her laugh could be heard all down the walkway. Billy leaned on Sara's arm while Sara bought the tickets.

Inside, it was pitch black and smelled of stables. A green ghost popped out from the right side, and a giant purple spider dropped in their path.

"Ugh!" Sara yelled.

A hall of mirrors distorted their bodies. Sara looked like a pear and Billy like a stick with a huge white cast. The path became soft and wavy. Billy clutched Sara's arm as they wobbled past a monster under glass and a fluorescent skeleton that dropped through a trap door.

"This is silly." Sara moved towards the exit.

"Now it's your turn," a voice boomed over their heads. Sara gasped. A wind machine roared full blast, blowing her off balance, throwing her against Billy. He clutched her. His cheek brushed hers. As the wind died down, his grasp loosened. Before Sara knew it, they were hugging. Then

Billy bent down and kissed her softly on the lips. Their eyes met briefly.

Sara darted into the sunlight, blinking. She rescued Billy's wheelchair from the ticket seller and pushed it right under Billy's knees so he dropped into it. Silence hung like a curtain between them.

Sara's head buzzed as she pushed Billy down the length of the midway.

"Stop here," Billy hollered as they passed the shooting gallery. He pulled himself to the counter and picked up a rifle. He shot at moving rabbits, targets and whirling wheels. It wasn't long before he held a giant panda out to Sara.

"Here," he said awkwardly.

"We've got to meet the others," was all Sara could manage to say before hurrying on.

* * *

"Sara, Billy, we're over here," a voice called over the din. It was Alice. Sara had forgotten all about the Island display.

Arthur clung to a ladder. He was taping up lists of supporters. The wind threatened to blow them down. Posters flapped in the stiff breeze from the lake. Quite a few Ward's Island people clustered around the booth.

"Where is everyone?" Sara asked.

"John Paul is at the kid's pavilion having a nap. Maggie and your mom have gone to the food building." Arthur leapt down from his perch.

"What have you two been up to?"

"Nothing," Billy said.

"Nothing," Sara said.

"Had a good time, eh," Arthur chuckled. "Okay, don't tell us. That's some nothing of a panda you've got, Sara." He winked at Alice.

Sara wandered over to look at all the stuff on the display table — handwoven scarves, watercolours, pottery, pressed wildflowers, homemade chocolates.

"I didn't know all this went on, did you?" Captain Joe stood behind the counter making change for a customer who was buying a teapot. "Here come Maggie and Ethel." Captain Joe pointed across the wide expanse of asphalt. Then he slapped his knee and looked towards the lakefront. "If I'm not at the dock later, go on without me. I've got to see a man about a boat." Captain Joe moved off.

"John Paul and I are going home right after supper," Ethel announced. "Fred's coming home tonight."

"Why don't you and I spend the rest of the evening together, *mo ghaoil*?" Maggie said to Sara.

"Good. Billy can go with the others," Sara said quickly.

"Boy trouble so soon?" Maggie laughed.

Sara scuffed her shoes in the small pebbles that rolled on the pavement. Her mother joined

117

them. A slight smile crinkled the corners of her steely blue eyes. "Your grandmother says you've been a great help this summer." She cleared her throat. "That's promising. I hope there's no more need for sneaky tricks."

Something in her mother's tone of voice stopped Sara — made her think, just for a moment, that she was not a little kid any more, that maybe she was to be trusted. Sara pulled her shoulders back and wet her lips.

"No more sneaky tricks. I promise."

Maggie, who had been sitting nearby, suddenly stood up. She winked at Sara, took Ethel's hand in her left hand, and reached for Sara's with her right. "How about one of the big spenders taking you two to dinner? Maybe we could talk about . . . " and she bit her lip, " . . . what to do with the Island house. I've got to let the Bests and Gladys know." Her voice trailed off. "And Captain Joe."

"Thank goodness." Ethel heaved a big sigh and turned John Paul's stroller around. "Could be a big load off my shoulders."

"Life's too short to spend it all worrying, Ethel. Spend some on yourself," Maggie scolded.

"You always say that, Mom," Ethel laughed. "Like a broken record."

"Trouble with old ladies, eh. We repeat ourselves."

15

After supper, Sara, wheeling Maggie, walked with her mom and John Paul back to the CNE gates. The baby's face still had traces of ice cream where Ethel had missed with a damp rag. He was gurgling and chatting to passing feet.

Ethel gave both Sara and Maggie her usual brisk hug. "See you Sunday morning." She pushed the cart through the turnstile and out to the parking lot. "Don't —"

"Stay out too late." Sara and Maggie finished the sentence together, laughing.

"Quick, if we hurry we can catch a ride on the speedy carousel." Sara pushed Maggie across the expanse of asphalt, past the throngs of visitors carrying balloons, candy floss and bags of souvenirs and samples or stuffing hot dogs or hamburgers into their mouths. Pigeons flapped and scurried near overflowing trash barrels. The boom of music from the rides carried across the gigantic fairground.

The sun was already fading in the western sky when Sara pulled onto the midway — to be greeted by Granny Pitts and Billy's dad.

"What a coincidence!" Mr. Best chuckled.

"A real coagulance!" echoed Granny Pitts. "Billy phoned and told us to meet him this afternoon. We've been having a grand time."

The four of them walked down the crowded skinny street past the games with names like "Toss the Hoop", "Guess Your Weight" and "Bowl Down Bunnies".

"Here come Alice and Arthur." Sara pointed as the pair approached, arm in arm, eating ice cream cones.

"Has anyone seen Billy?" Arthur hollered. "He was going to meet us by the carousel." The whole of the menagerie giggled and shoved and hugged like they hadn't seen each other since forever.

"Wait for me, you guys," a voice shouted from the sky. Sara looked up. There was Billy Best, cast and all, riding on the giant ferris wheel with Kevin the deck-hand.

"Wait until you see what Captain Joe's got," Kevin hollered.

After Billy and Kevin joined them, they passed the little kiddie carousel and headed for the biggest, oldest carousel in the park. As they approached the ticket booth, Kevin said, "There used to be one faster at Sunnyside. But now this is the fastest carousel there is."

Arthur bought tickets for Sara, Maggie, Alice and himself. Mr. Best bought them for his family, and Kevin bought his own. "I wish Captain Joe would hurry up. I can't sit on the news all night, can you, Billy?" he said.

Sara was busy finding the horse she wanted to ride. It had to be on the outside, on the fast track. Granny Pitts sat on the inside on one of the benches. Billy had to sit with her, his cast propped up on the seat ahead.

As Sara weaved her way along the rows of black, brown and red horses, Maggie called, "Ride the palomino. That's the one I'd choose." Sure enough a beautiful tan and white dappled horse, with light, shiny eyes and a flowing blonde mane, stood out in the row of bigger horses.

Maggie had decided to be sensible, she said. She sat wrapped in her coat by the ticket booth, with the waiting parents, waving as Sara flew by. The carousel, sounding like a giant music box, played "Love is a Many Splendoured Thing".

Sara glanced around her. Most of the people she loved were right here, ringed around her. Alice and Arthur were riding side by side on a pair of matched grey mares. Behind her, Mr. Best was draped over a giant black stallion with flaming red eyes. Kevin was laughing and hanging on backwards to a brown mare with a wide rear end.

Suddenly there was a commotion at the gate. Captain Joe, in his off-duty jeans and pea jacket, was pushing through the crowd of parents. He jumped on the moving carousel, and planted a kiss on Sara's forehead.

He swung around and around one of the brass poles in the centre row. All the kids, big and little, turned and stared at him. "I bought it! I bought it!" he shouted. "And I've got you to thank for the idea, Sara Jane." The captain threw her another kiss and leaped onto the back of a spotted pony.

Sara scratched her chin with her free hand. What was Captain Joe talking about? What had he bought? Probably a barrel of mussels or herring. She was too busy riding up and down, going round and round, faster and faster as the carousel speeded up to pay much attention to Captain Joe. Maggie was a wavery blur on the sidelines. This merry-go-round was faster than any she'd ever ridden on. Wow!

"Oh, dearie me." Granny Pitts. "What ancilleration."

"Acceleration, Grandma." Billy gave his grandma a little nudge.

"That's what I said, didn't I?"

As the song ended, the carousel slowed. Sara hung on tight to the pole in her hand. She felt dizzy, but good. The whole day had worked out

— even though she'd blabbed to the doctor and her mother had come. She sighed.

She clambered off the ride and joined the menagerie gathered around Maggie and Captain Joe. "I want all of you to follow me down to the docks. I've got a little surprise for you," the captain was saying. His eyes glistened like the stars that were beginning to appear in the early evening sky. He reached across and tapped Sara on the shoulder. "I want you to come for sure."

The whole gang made their way down to the waterfront, where the boat races and aquatic events were held. Captain Joe led the way, pushing Maggie in her chair, talking to beat the band. Maggie smiled and pulled her coat around her. There was quite a breeze blowing off the lake.

"She'll need a little work, you realize. And I'll have to change her name. Some spit and polish and tender loving care and she'll outshine all the others on the lagoon."

"What?" Sara kept asking, but he wouldn't answer.

He stopped by the waterfront, turned and swept his arm to his left. A tidy little sloop, its white sail rolled up neatly and its cabin windows shuttered, rode gently on the incoming waves. "She's not the *Trillium*, but she'll give a smooth ride, and a berth for summer nights."

Just as the menagerie began shouting their congratulations — Crash! Bang! Shwoosh! — the first of the evening's fireworks filled the sky with sound and light.

"Come on, gang. We'll miss the ferry!" Arthur motioned, and the motley crew, still yelling their good wishes, waved and hurried off to the parking lot.

Sara and Maggie were the last to leave the dock.

"I'm going to call her the MS *Little Trillium*, Maggie," Captain Joe called after them. "That's Marine Sloop or Maggie Shaw's *Little Trillium*, take your pick!" He took his pipe out of his pocket and knocked it on the railing by the dock. As Maggie and Sara hurried after the menagerie, he filled it with fresh tobacco, lit it, then dropped over the side to sit in the stern of his new home.

16

Bright and early Sunday morning, Sara woke to the singing of birds. A flock of sparrows flew past her open window, close enough that the sound of their wings blended with the crash of the waves. Sara put on her favourite outfit, worn jeans that rode high on her calves, she had grown so much. She pulled on old red socks. One of them had a hole in the toe. All the better for what she was about to do.

She grabbed a couple of oatcakes, slapped some grape jam in the middle, gulped down a glass of ice cold milk and tiptoed to the door. As she passed the screened porch she glanced in. Maggie's braided rug was draped over two card tables. It was finished.

Sara swallowed the last bite of oatcake sandwich and went in to look at it. She took in the tiny stitches, the range of colors, the feel of all those fabrics. Stuff from Maggie's life, her own mom's dresses and scarves, her dad's old ties, her dead uncle's pilot's uniform, her grandpa's velvet smoking jacket. The material felt nubbly and warm. There was a scrap from Sara's first dress, the old green knee sock that she had worn the first day of school. And here, close to the end, splotches of paisley from the cotton dress Maggie had been wearing at the beginning of the summer, the one that finally swam on her, she'd lost so much weight.

The old suitcase on the floor held a jumble of leftover bits and pieces barely covering the bottom of the case. Sara looked them over. That's when she spotted the masking tape tag on the end table. *E.C.*, it said. The Chinese-lady lamp had a patch of masking tape, too. It said *A. and A.* Sara crawled across the floor to the old wicker chair. *Store* was scrawled on a piece of sticky tape. The leg of the coffee table had another *E.C.* on it. *E.C.* were her mother's initials. What was going on here?

Sara lifted the corner of the rag rug to look at the card table. *E.C.*, again, this time in a red scrawl. A big hunk of tape was fastened to the bottom of the rag rug. *For S.J.C.* it said.

She dropped the rug quickly and backed out of the room, bumping into the refrigerator. It snapped on, humming and gurgling. Sara dashed out the door and down the walk to the lakeshore.

The screen door banged as she turned the corner.

Not a soul was on the beach. Only Sara and the birds, the sweeping gulls, the cheeping chickadees, bold jays and timid sparrows. What were her initials doing on the rug?

Sara walked slowly down the lakefront to the eastern end of the breakwater. A light morning mist hung over the horizon. She made her way across the sand to the long straight line of giant rocks and stones that rose up from the beach like a looming shadow. Amongst the granite and sandstone were jagged, black boulders covered with lime-green seaweed, barnacles and sea creatures. A lone white gull screeched as Sara stood stock-still, staring the length of the breakwater. The gull, flapping its wings, swept ahead of her, floated above the line of rocks and suddenly veered off towards the deep water and the invisible shores to the south. The bird's wings shone in the filtered sun.

With arms outstretched on either side, Sara sprang along the rocks. She gritted her teeth in concentration. She whistled as she moved swiftly down the line of rocks with the thundering waves to her left and the calm green water to her right. A strong wind was coming up, so strong it might blow her over.

She grabbed for a hunk of granite with one hand and leapt for a boulder. Her left foot skidded out from under her. *No, I won't fall in,* she thought. "I've got good balance," she shouted into the air around her. A fish jumped, startling her, but still she didn't slip.

As she clambered and climbed down the rocks towards the western end of the breakwater, Sara could feel her heart inside her chest, heaving and beating, rhythmic and strong. She was going to make it.

"Sara! Sara!" A voice ahead was flung her way by the same wind that buffeted her. She nearly lost her footing, looking up, angry at the interruption.

Billy stood on crutches on the water's edge by the end of the breakwater, waving madly. "You're out of your mind, out here alone. You could have fallen in. Your dad's here."

Sara pulled her foot, which was hovering over the stormy waters on the lake side, back to safety, to solid rock. Then she sprinted, leaping rock to rock to the end of the breakwater where she jumped into the cool water and swam to shore.

"I did it! I did it!" She shook herself like a woolly dog and ran down the street towards the house on Hiawatha Street, leaving Billy struggling on his own.

"Where have you been, this hour of the morning? You're all wet!" Arthur, busy making pancakes and bacon with Alice, looked up as she hurried in the back door.

"Shh!" Sara ran up the back stairs to her room. She towelled down quickly, put on fresh clothes, pulled a comb through her hair and ran back downstairs.

"Here she is. Here's Sara!" Her mom was sitting on the couch beside Maggie.

Her dad strode across the room and folded her into his arms. "I brought my fishing gear."

Granny Pitts had John Paul on her lap. She was trying to get the teddy bear sweater on him.

Captain Joe and Mr. Best were going over the blueprints of his sailboat. "We'll take her out for a spin after brunch, shall we?" The Captain's bushy eyebrows puckered and waved. His pipe lay forgotten in the ashtray.

Gladys sat drinking black coffee. "I read where a whole family disappeared in a sailboat in the south seas. Not a trace was ever found of any of them or their boat."

The rag rug lay rolled up in the corner by the closed suitcase.

"My mother has an announcement." Sara's mother's voice boomed over the chattering crowd.

Alice and Arthur came to the doorway, carrying platters of pancakes and bacon, eggs and sausages, hash browns and baked tomatoes.

Maggie began. "As most of you already know, I've been on the Island every summer since Joe Shaw died. Summers in the city seemed so hot

129

and close. Here, with all my friends around me, summers flew by."

"Time changes things." Maggie blinked, pulled at the locket around her neck. "I'm letting the lease go to Metro next month." Gladys gasped. Granny Pitts held John Paul so tight he squealed.

"Some of you won't be too surprised." Maggie looked at Captain Joe, the blueprints of his boat firmly clasped in his hands.

The room fell silent. Maggie's hands in her lap trembled.

"Let's eat this before it becomes stone cold in the market," Arthur chimed in.

"Have you read *Gone with the Wind* by Tide L. Wave?" Billy was greeted by a chorus of groans.

"Some things don't change." Maggie blinked back tears.

Sara stood with her arm around her dad's waist, watching the whole menagerie line up, plates in hand, filing past the table laden with food.

"How was your summer, Sara?" he whispered as the two of them sauntered over to the end of the line. Her mother was busy filling Maggie's plate and taking it to her.

Sara told him about bird-watching, and following old Quantz, about the trip to the CNE, and walking the breakwater without falling off.

She piled her plate high with good food and found a seat, on the footstool by Grandma's feet.

The phone rang. Sara jumped for it, nearly knocking over her whole plate.

"Sara, you've the grace of an elephant," her mom said.

Sara sighed and picked up the phone. Like Billy and his jokes, some things never change.

"Long distance for Maggie Shaw," the line crackled. "It's California calling."

Sara dropped the receiver. "Quick, Maggie, it's California."

"Oh, my! Oh, my!" Maggie rose and lurched toward the phone. "It's my dearies." Her cheeks grew pink. She clutched the phone as if it were in danger of floating away. " 'Tis *mo choineachain*."

"Hello!" she shouted,

"You don't have to holler, Grandma. Long distance phones work fine." Arthur gave Maggie a little hug as he danced by to flip more pancakes.

"It's a matter of electrohomes." Granny Pitts dipped a piece of pancake in syrup and handed it to John Paul.

"Electronics," Billy corrected her.

Now Mom was sharing the phone with Maggie, talking to her sisters. "Imagine you three getting together and figuring we'd all be here on Labour Day weekend. Oh, you tried the house first."

Sara popped the last bite of sausage into her mouth and went and stood beside her mom and grandma. The three of them clustered around the phone. Suddenly the receiver was thrust into her hand. "Say 'Hi' to your aunts."

"Ethel says you might come and see us sometime. Pick a peck of oranges," one aunt said. Her voice sounded like she was talking through cotton batting.

"Let us talk to Maggie again. Bye, Sara," another aunt said.

Sara wandered back to sit down beside her dad.

"I guess I'll just have to stay in the city from now on," Gladys was saying, puffing on a cigarette.

"My son-in-law is looking at a house on Ward's." said Mrs. Pitts. "The owner wants to sublet it. Captain Joe has the *Little Trillium* to sleep on and sail. He'll park on the lagoon."

Alice and Arthur cleared the table. Sara pitched in to help. For some reason she felt like crying, like running down to the beach.

Alice put a hand on her arm, and looked into her eyes. "That was a great thing you did, Sara, taking your grandma to the CNE. She had a good time."

Sara puckered her face.

"Hey, kid, next year you could come and stay with us over on Ward's, you know. We'll be married by then!" Arthur danced Sara around the room.

"I'm probably going to California, with my dad and mom and John Paul, and Maggie."

"So? You won't be gone for the whole summer. Besides, Billy will need someone to keep him in line. Won't you, Billy?"

"You just want me to deliver flyers, save birds, stop wars," Billy said, grinning. "Come on, Sara, let's get out of here."

Sara plopped on the swing and Billy gingerly collapsed into the hammock with a moan.

"Too bad you can't come fishing." Sara pumped like blazes until her toes were hitting the bottom leaves on the horse chestnut tree. The ropes squawked as she rode high. "With my dad and me."

17

Sara and her dad spent most of the day out on the wide lagoon, their lines trailing in the water, talking about school and teaching, and wondering when John Paul would be big enough to come along.

"He's more like a real person. I kinda like him," Sara said. Her line jiggled. "I got a bite. I got a bite."

"Give the fish a little line to play with. Take your time. Easy now. " It was a bass, a big shiny one, its sides sparkling in the sun. The fish flopped back and forth and back and forth, trying to get its mouth away from the hook.

All the others they had caught had been too small to keep. Her dad took the hook out, and dropped the bass into a bucket filled with water. The fish bumped its nose up against the sides. Sara stared at him, alone and swimming. Poor dumb thing.

"We should head back pretty soon. Your mother will be getting anxious." Her dad sighed. "It's good to be home."

Sara kept staring at the lone bass in the bucket.

"I guess there's a few bites on him," her dad mused.

Sara gazed at the fish again. The fish stared back. Sara made her decision. She leaned over, lifted the bucket handle and tossed the bass and the water back into the lagoon.

Her dad stopped rowing and turned to watch the bubbles on the surface as the fish disappeared.

"Wouldn't have made a meal, would he?" Sara mumbled, putting her hands on the gunnels. "All alone like that."

As they pulled down the leeside of the channel, Captain Joe, with Billy and Mr. Best, Arthur and Kevin, came putt-putting along, back from a spin in the sailboat. Sara clambered on board as both boats docked.

"Wow! It's as big as a cruiser. Gee, Captain Joe."

"I know, you'll have to go for a ride real soon. Next, maybe. I'm taking Maggie out later today. She's a little nervous, I think. She's not been on a sailboat since she left Scotland." And then he scratched his head. "Kept talking about how if the sails are tacking to the west, out into the open sea, the boat is headed for the other shore. That's silly — we can't sail all the way to the States, not this afternoon."

Sara's dad cleared his throat. "If I remember right, the Celts believe that when folks die their bodies are carried away to the west, to islands they can't see, islands beyond the horizon."

Suddenly Sara was running down the sidewalk, towards the house on Hiawatha Street, back to Maggie.

The house was silent. Her mother sat reading on the couch and looked up as Sara entered. "Back already?" John Paul stirred, dozing in his carriage in the corner of the room.

"Where's Maggie?" Sara asked, rushing out to the kitchen, listening for gurgling pipes.

"She's napping, Sara. Leave her be." Her mother patted the couch beside her. "We had a good long talk, Maggie and me, while you were off gallivanting. She showed me her bank book and her will, and a page of instructions about all the legal matters. She's really put some thought into the future."

"Have you checked on her, Mom?" Sara could feel her muscles tighten, the blood pound in her chest. "How long has she been asleep, Mom? She only dozes, off and on." Sara tiptoed down the hall. Her mother came behind her. The two of them stood outside the door. Sara strained to hear the whistle-snore. There wasn't a sound.

She opened the door to Maggie's room slowly. Her hand shook on the doorknob.

Maggie lay on the bed, under a white comforter for extra warmth. Her eyes were closed. The room was quiet. Sara stared at her grandmother's peaceful face. There was something missing. What was missing?

"Mother! Mother!" Ethel was leaning over Maggie, calling softly. "Time to wake up."

Sara stopped in her tracks. She'd been walking around the other side of the bed. Why wasn't her grandmother snoring? Why wasn't that funny little whuffle-whistle rattling her grandma's chest, ruffling her lips?

"Sara, run outside. Sara, run and get your father. Sara, run away." Her mother's voice climbed higher, louder with each phrase.

Sara didn't move. Instead, she planted her feet firm. She looked at the motionless woman on the bed, and at her mother, dropped now beside the bed, holding onto one white hand, the other pale white hand lying on the cover. Sara's head throbbed. She shut her eyes, screwed them tight and opened them again. Her grandmother lay as still as ever, her white hair framing her face on the pink pillowcase. A crossword puzzle and a pencil were on the floor beside the bed. Sara picked them up, lay them on the bedside table, knelt beside the bed and took her grandmother's other hand.

It was cold. Her grandmother was dead.

"We're back!" Her dad's voice boomed from the kitchen. Sara's mother sprang to her feet and hurried from the room.

"You knew, didn't you, Maggie? You knew you were going away." Sara leaned on the bed, her head in her hands, until she felt her dad's arms lifting her, guiding her out the door, down the hall, and into the living room, where she sat, stunned and empty.

* * *

Later, after the doctor had come, after the funeral directors had taken the body away, after sandwiches and tea and everyone sitting around on the porch telling stories, Sara took John Paul in her arms.

"You know, she spoke the Gaelic this morning," Ethel was saying. "Something like, '*Tha gu math, mo ghaoil, tha gu math*'."

"I think she was saying she was all right, my dears," Arthur said.

"Sounds like Maggie." Alice came through the door and stood close to Arthur.

"Come on, John Paul, I'll change your diaper." Sara said to the baby.

She left the grownups going over the details again. She didn't want to hear. Every detail burned in her brain as it was.

"Boy, you show no respect for serious occasions." She held her nose as she swished John

Paul's dirty diaper in the toilet. She pulled the blinds down and handed him his bottle. He lay in her old crib staring up at Sara with wide eyes.

"You probably won't remember her." Sara let the tears flow down her cheeks. "And I will never forget."

John Paul's eyes were closing.

"I wish I'd had a chance to say goodbye." Sara sighed and wiped the tears from her face.

"We're going to the funeral home to make arrangements," Arthur called from the bottom of the stairs.

"Keep an eye on John Paul, will you?" Her mother pulled her coat and hat on.

Sara jumped. *Keep an eye on* . . . She had failed, hadn't she? She had come to the Island to keep an eye on Maggie. And her grandmother was dead.

18

On Saturday, three weeks later, Sara woke and stared around her room on Dufferin Street. The traffic noise wasn't as bad as usual. She lay listening to the faint husha-husha of tires on the road, the cry of a distant siren, the gurgling of her baby brother in his crib in the next room.

She heaved a big sigh. She still cried at night when no one could hear her, when she was alone in her room. She kept expecting to see Maggie coming in the door, or to find her sitting on the porch. She'd been back to school and everyone said how sorry they felt, but most of them hadn't known Maggie. Susan, her best friend, said Sara was acting like a zombie. It felt more like living under water. Everything seemed far away.

Leaning in the corner, wrapped in a roll of butcher paper, taller than a pole on the carousel, was Maggie's rag rug.

Sara climbed out of bed and put her feet on the cold linoleum floor. Maggie had meant her to put the rug down there, to keep her feet warm, but she hadn't been able to do it. Not yet.

"Sara, come on." Her dad's voice rose up the stairwell.

Sara dragged her work clothes on slowly. She dawdled tying her running shoes.

"Sara?"

"Coming, Dad."

Mom was making toast. John Paul banged his spoon, and laughed up at his sister as she walked into the spotless kitchen.

"Billy, Mr. Best, Arthur and Alice will be here with the van any minute." Her dad handed her a glass of orange juice.

Her mother hadn't said anything. In fact, her mother hadn't said much since Maggie's funeral. She hadn't worried about Sara's slow dishwashing or staying up late. Maybe if she'd give her heck, they'd both feel better.

"We'll move the piano first, Ethel." Sara's dad walked into the front room. "Where do you want it?"

Her mother was carrying dishes to the sink. She laid them on the counter without a sound. Then she gripped the edge of the sink with both hands. Sara watched her mother's knuckles whiten.

"Ethel, where do you want the piano?" Sara's dad called again.

Sara bit her lip. She looked around the room for something to do, tried to think of something to say. She got up and walked over to the white sink, stood beside her mother, put her hand on top of her mother's hand.

"Go on, Mom." She gulped. "Go tell Dad where to put the piano, okay?"

Her mother slowly uncurled her fingers from the cold porcelain, then wiped her hands on her apron. Sara thought she saw a hint of tears in her mother's eyes.

Sara finished the dishes and heated the pot for tea, pouring a big cup for both her mom and dad. When they came back into the kitchen, they sat at the table. Her mother's face had some of its colour back. She'd put on fresh lipstick.

She reached across the table and patted Sara's hand. "Thanks," she said. "Thanks for making the tea."

* * *

Over at the Island, the menagerie was putting boxes into the van. Arthur had permission to run a vehicle onto the Island for the day while they loaded everything up from Maggie's house. He and Alice had already packed the dishes and bedding and had held a little rummage sale, giving most of the leftovers to the Salvation Army and Maggie's church.

While Billy, Arthur, Mr. Best and Sara's dad moved stuff, Sara sat on the porch with Alice.

"How's it going, kid?"

"Okay," Sara said, without thinking about it.

"I really mean it. How's it going?" Alice's long brown hair hung down, hiding her face. She had a funny peasant skirt on. "Now that I'm back teaching kindergarten kids, I realize how big you are. I really like big kids."

Sara made a hole in the grass with the toe of her running shoe. She pressed her hands down her legs and took a deep breath.

"Do you think the trip to the CNE did it?"

Alice didn't say anything for a minute. "Is that what you think?"

"I just wondered. Maybe . . . "

Alice leaned closer, put her arm around Sara's shoulders. Sara couldn't help herself. Her shoulders started shaking. Pretty soon, her whole body was shaking, as if she'd been holding it together by wearing clothes, by going to school, by doing dishes. She gulped twice, in the midst of her tears. She felt really stupid.

"It's okay, Sara. I've cried plenty and she wasn't even my grandma." The two of them stood and strolled down the block away from the house, the house with its echoing rooms and its packed furniture, down to the lakefront.

Alice picked up a flat stone from the beach and heaved it towards the breakwater.

Sara picked one up too and tossed it as hard as she could. It bounced four times and sank.

"Do you think she knew?" Sara called over the sound of the waves. "Maybe I shouldn't have taken her to the CNE." She picked up a fat rock and tossed it, listening as it chunked over the surface of the water.

"Some things we'll never know," Alice said. "We know she wanted to go to the CNE. We know she had a good time. We all did, didn't we?"

Sara nodded her head, wiped her eyes with her sleeve. Alice smiled at her. "Race you?" she called and headed back towards Hiawatha Street. Sara passed her as they turned the corner, in time to see Arthur banging the van door.

"The swing, don't forget the swing. We don't want Quantz selling it." Billy shinnied up the tree, proud that his leg was out of its cast and working well again, and undid the ropes. Sara hauled the swing with her down the street as they trudged after the packed van. She turned as they came close to the canoe club. The top leaves on some of the trees were already turning yellow. Fall was coming — Sara's summer was over.

Back on Hiawatha Street, the house looked sad with no curtains, no deck chairs out front. It reminded Sara of the way her grandma had looked lying in bed that last day — like no one was there any more. The house needed someone in it to make it lively. She ran to catch up to Billy.

"So, do you want to go to a movie next Saturday or not?" he asked.

"Maybe."

He punched her arm.

"No kissing," she said.

"No kissing."

They got to the dock after the van had pulled onto the deck of the ferry and parked. Everyone trooped to the upper deck to watch the *Thomas Rennie* cast off.

"I forgot to say goodbye to Captain Joe," Sara gasped.

Arthur laughed. "He's too busy setting forth on his own. He and Kevin are taking the *Little Trillium* on her first major journey. Took a whole crate of herring, too."

"Yuck," said Billy. *"The Case of the Stinking Cargo* by Joe N.S. Crate."

Sara ignored him and stared out at the harbour. Gulls swooped and soared. A tug passed, tooting its horn. Behind it, attached by giant ropes, slipped the grand old *Trillium*, moving slowly towards the Island.

Billy raised his binoculars, leaned out and swept them along the length of the old ferry.

Sara grabbed the binoculars from him. "Let me see."

She focussed the glasses, then swept the deck of the *Trillium*. She'd been stripped of her benches and lifejackets. She was deserted. Wait!

The cat was riding on the prow, sitting straight and tall.

"Wow! That dumb old cat. She's riding the *Trillium*. Without a ticket, too." Sara laughed, hard and loud.

"I don't see what's so funny," Billy said. Looking at Sara's stricken face, he added quickly, "I want you to keep those binoculars. I'd been planning on giving them to you." He ran down the stairs to the other end of the inner cabin.

Sara stayed where she was. Arthur and Alice were sitting together on the deck behind her. So was Mr. Best. Maybe Alice was right, thought Sara. Maybe Maggie would have died anyway. Maybe the trip to the CNE had nothing to do with it. She felt dizzy, suddenly. She gripped the railing and put the binoculars to her eyes one more time. The *Trillium* had disappeared behind the trees, into the lagoon.

Back in the harbour, a small sailboat was making its way towards open water, its white sail whuffling in the wind. Sara adjusted the binoculars once more, this time to catch some sign of life on the little craft.

She could see two dark figures, one pulling on ropes and the other handling the steering. She shifted the glasses a trifle, to catch the name on the back of the sloop.

The MS *Little Trillium*. Maggie Shaw's *Little*

Trillium was heading out of the harbour, full speed ahead.

Sara waved like crazy. "Goodbye," she sang out. "Goodbye."

Alice jumped up, borrowed the glasses and took a good long look. Then Arthur grabbed the glasses from her.

The small white sailboat rode high on the waves as she headed away from them, her sails fluttering like birds' wings, catching the wind, riding the currents out and away across the horizon.

Long after the others had gone downstairs, Sara stood waving, watching the tiny boat slip through the gap and journey out of sight. Only then did she let go of the wooden railing and make her way over to the iron steps down to the gangplank. Only then did she turn her face towards the city. She took a deep breath of harbour air — fishy, watery, with a touch of oil and cinders. It was time she went home.

Sara flew down the steps and across the dock to the van. When she got to Dufferin Street, she'd have to unroll Maggie's rug and put it on her floor. It would keep her feet warm on cool fall mornings. She could stretch out on it with a pillow and read books.

She might even start saving some scraps of her own.

The *Trillium* lay in the Island lagoon for seventeen years. It was rehabilitated in the 1970's and returned to service in 1976. The homes on Centre and Algonquin Islands were all demolished by the mid-sixties, and replaced with parks. Ward Islanders continued to resist for another twenty years. As of 1990, some two hundred homes still stand there.